Teaching School

Points Picked Up

A book for anyone who is teaching, wants to teach, or knows a teacher

by
Eric W. Johnson

National Association of Independent Schools
4 Liberty Square, Boston, Massachusetts 02109

Illustrations by Howard S. L. Coale

Library of Congress Cataloging in Publication Data
Johnson, Eric W.
   Teaching school.

   Includes index.
   1. Teaching. 2. Curriculum planning. 3. Lesson planning. I. Title.
LB1025.2.J614   371.1'02   79-9352
ISBN 0-934338-39-6

To the hundreds of teachers, good and bad,
and the thousands of students, taught and mistaught,
who have given me points picked up.

Contents

Preface

Some cynic said, "Education is casting false pearls before real swine." Well, perhaps, in a few places, with a few people. But to me teaching is as noble, challenging, stimulating, and rewarding a job as one can set one's heart and mind to — except on Fridays and during the month of February.

There are about 2.5 million schoolteachers in the United States and Canada, over 150,000 of them new to their jobs each year. It seems to me that many of them, both the experienced and the new, will be helped by a brief, practical, middle-of-the-road book of suggestions on how to teach school. As far as I can tell (and I've recently read through more than 200 books on teaching), no good book of this sort now exists, and so I've tried to write one.

I have been a teacher for about 30 years and have also performed various administrative tasks. Since spending four years as principal (1948 to 1952), I have been climbing steadily down the administrative ladder and have spent most of my time as a mere classroom teacher, which is not so mere. My own children have finished school, thus freeing me to pontificate without fear of contradiction by reality. I even consult with schools now and then, when someone wants me to advise them or hear their problems.

As I go about in both public and private schools, I see not a few teachers who seem to be leading overstimulating lives of not so quiet desperation. I see others who have become habit-ridden, characterized by toleration of circumstances they see as unchangeable, and who respond with boredom and resigned adjustment, not untinged with cynicism. Still others, perhaps the largest number, are trying energetically and successfully to do a good job. They keep their enthusiasm and their self-confidence but are always on the lookout for ways to do better.

I sense that most teachers, both the new and the experienced, are healthily convinced that they are giving their all in hard and important work and that they welcome all practical ideas for even better ways to teach and any workable suggestions for how to stand up under the strains of the job without withdrawing from its responsibilities — and without having to foment revolutions.

Most of those 200 books on teaching I read fall into one of two categories. One group brilliantly promotes a radical point of view or method that has worked for two or three years of system-defying, life-flinging effort on the part of the author before he or she left the classroom and took to the typewriter. The other group dully expounds, at length and ploddingly, in textbook format, the elements of education, with lists of objectives, overviews, sections and subsections, summaries and study questions, usually printed two columns per page on glossy paper.

I did, however, discover one really crisp, readable, practical book on school teaching: *Points Picked Up: One Hundred Hints in How To Manage a School*, by Abbie G. Hall. Unfortunately, since it was published about 90 years ago (1891), it's a little out of date, and I'm sorry that Abbie Hall is not alive today to revise it. But the book is full of what is good sense, and from it I have taken part of the title of my book, *Points Picked Up*.

Abbie Hall's first hint is "Begin school as if you had just heard good news and took pleasure in imparting, and keep this up all day," and her last, number 116, not 100, is, "Honor your School Board that your days may be long in the land in which you are teaching." I use a Hall hint as introduction to each of the first 24 chapters in this book and have reproduced all 116 of Abbie Hall's hints in the Appendix.

My book is not as slim as Miss Hall's, but I hope it is as straightforward and practical. For teachers who are new to the classroom, it provides suggestions on how to combine eagerness for the job, knowledge of subject, and enjoyment of kids into good teaching while avoiding some unnecessary pains and pitfalls along the way. For the experienced, or the tired, or the discouraged, I hope it may suggest some fresh ideas, new perspectives, and examples of how to improve or enrich their teaching.

I have not hesitated to pronounce without apology. All teachers worth their salt will reject what won't work for them or in their school, and, as Oliver Wendell Holmes said, "An apology is only egotism wrong side out." Where an opinion is needed, I give one because a sensible opinion is usually better than none, especially if no one forces it upon you. If you disagree with the opinion, ignore it. I agree with Mark Twain that "loyalty to petrified opinion never yet broke a chain or freed a human soul."

E. W. J.

1.
Order

Hint 84. Do not scold and never threaten.   *Abbie G. Hall*

A few years ago, I asked 400 boys and girls in grades 5-9 in public and private schools some questions about themselves, their homes, and their schools. One of my questions was, "What are the most important qualities of a good teacher?"

The ten qualities they mentioned most often, in order of frequency, were, "Nice, kind, helpful," "Strict, firm, in control," "Interesting, makes learning fun," "Understanding," "Keeps good balance between control and freedom," and "Relates well to students." Note well the first three, which have to do with the first three chapters of this book: spirit, order, interest.

To give you a feel for how the students expressed themselves, here are a few verbatim quotations on the subject of a good teacher: "Is harsh and gentle at the right times," "Is serious when it is time to be serious and clowns around when it is time to clown around," "Is not an old square goat," "Thinks before yelling," "Doesn't teach all by control," "Shows no wishywashyness," "Doesn't inflict personal opinions on the class," "Teaches you to learn from your mistakes," "Is forceful in the subjects but agreeable to the kids," "Knows about a young mind," and "Gets ideas from the class so she can improve herself."

I also asked, "What are the most important characteristics of a poor teacher?" They were, listed in the same manner, "Can't keep order," "Boring," "Yells, gets angry easily," "Unfair, has favorites," "Mean, not helpful," "Doesn't know subject," and

"Lacks intelligence." Again, note well the first three: order, interest, and an aspect of spirit.

Here are some verbatim comments about the poor teacher: "Lets the kids do whatever they want," "Is grinding — too powerful, rules the kids like prisoners," "Stops talking whenever there's the slightest noise," "Treats you like animals," "Doesn't explain things," "Never stops explaining things," "Is too quick and rushy," "Is not willing to face up to the students' criticisms," "Cries in class," "Is intolerant of mistakes," "Covers up own mistakes," "Is always trying to find the bad in what kids do," and "Just wants money."

Probably all teachers, experienced or novice, exhibit some of these qualities and characteristics at some point during a year, or even a week, of teaching. In the evening after one of our better days (or, if we are strong, after one of our worse days) at school, it might not be a bad idea for each of us to go down the items on these lists, construing each of them as a query to ourselves — "Was I forceful in the subjects but agreeable to the kids?" "Did I think before yelling?" — and see how we rate.

Certainly, the main elements of teaching — order, interest, spirit, and, we must add a fourth, discipline — are as inseparable from and dependent on one another as fire, water, air, and earth were to the ancients as the building materials of the universe. However, to clarify some matters and to give some workable suggestions for teaching, I am going to treat the elements one at a time, in the first four chapters, starting here with order.

Order vs. chaos

In every school and in every classroom, order is better than chaos, even though there are times when permitted chaos can be extremely educational. While order for its own sake is a pale virtue, every classroom does need a backbone of order to hold up the marvelous body of learning, with all its organs and systems.

It's best to have a clear idea what the backbone of order in your classroom is going to be well before school starts and, with your students' help, to start erecting it the first day. It is far easier to relax a fair system of orderliness later on than it is to start with chaotic bits and bursts, even accompanied by the friendliest of intentions, and then try to assemble from the wreckage some workable structure of order that will permit good learning to take place. You have a big advantage the first day. If you don't use it, you may feel like the distressed new third-grade teacher who said, "Teaching is like trying to hold 35 corks under water all at once."

Order in upper grades

In upper grades, where the students usually come to you for only a single period, it is essential to have classroom routines clearly thought out in advance and to explain them early. Here are some suggestions.

● Write your name on the board and be sure that the students know how they are to address you — "Mr. Johnson," "Eric," "Sir," or whatever else the school custom is. Don't try to be popular by asking them to call you by your first name when all those other people you might like to consider stuffy insist on "Mr.," "Miss," "Mrs.," or "Ms." On the other hand, you do have two names, so don't be overteacherly and just write "Mr. Johnson."

● Quietly but audibly indicate where students are to sit or tell them they may sit wherever they wish.

● When all are present, wait for the class to be quiet and then explain or say whatever you've planned. Don't shout over a noisy class, except to say that it's time to start. Better than shouting is just to look pregnant with utterance so that the class will quiet down to hear what's going to come out. If this doesn't work, a vigorous, friendly "Class!" will do.

● Explain and carry out roll-taking procedures. Once you know the students' names, you can take the roll as they come in or simply notice early in the period who is absent. When meeting a class for the first time, let the students say their names so that you will know how to pronounce them; then say them back.

● It is vital to learn everybody's name (and preferred nickname, if any), even if it takes a while. One good way to do this is to make a seating chart and mark each student's name by his place, asking students to sit in the same place every day until you know all their names. With a chart, you can call them all by their names the first day. "Linda, please . . ." is much more effective than "Hey, you . . ."

• As soon as necessary, explain procedures for handing out materials and collecting papers and make them as simple as possible.

• Have something on the board to engage the attention of all the students the moment they come into the room, headed, "To Do as Soon as You are Seated." Examples: "Write down 5-10 actions you observed between entering the school grounds and now. Try to choose actions that you think most people did not see"; "Open your book to page 37 and do the first exercise"; "Look around the room and write down several ways you think it could be improved"; "Write freely and quickly exactly how you are feeling right now." It's always good to have something ready for everyone to do in case you are delayed or have something important to attend to before speaking to the entire class.

• Explain that you expect people who raise their hands to have something to say and to be recognized by you before speaking, so that each may be heard and all who want may have a turn. Stick firmly to this procedure until you and the class agree to modify it.

• If you are new to the school, find out from the old pros what the systems are, learn them, and apply them in a firm and friendly manner. Later, you may want to change things in your room, but early in the school year know the systems and use them. You can be quite sure that most of the students will know them. If you and the students are familiar with the school and its routines, the best way to begin the first period is to launch right into the subject of the class or course.

The best general approach to routines, I've found, is a brief, clear explanation and the expectation that it will be understood and followed. Always be open to reasonable questions about procedures, however, and ready to change them if the change makes sense and doesn't go against any established school practices.

Order deliberately challenged

Occasionally, a student, or even a class, will start the year determined to test the teacher, especially a new one. Does he have authority? Can she manage things? Can we have some fun at the teacher's expense?

When students come bent on contest, you can avoid a lot of grief if you make sure that you win — not by putting them down, or making them feel bad about themselves, or rubbing in your victory — but by seeing to it that the reasonable expectations of order, consideration, and teaching prevail over the will to disruption. How can you win? By explaining firmly, without losing your cool, why you require whatever it may be. Don't call down the entire class, but deal with one of the prime movers, by name and in a friendly, definite, businesslike way. Try to avoid being an adversary; let it be a student's behavior, as measured against common-sense expectations, rather than the student against you. For example, say, "There's no way you can learn biology this year if you can't hear instructions," rather than, "I won't have you talking when I'm trying to talk."

If you think it will work, back off from the one-to-one contest and say something like, "OK, class, we're obviously not getting anywhere this way. What's the problem?" and let them discuss it, one speaking at a time, with emphasis on what kinds of behavior will solve the problem. But don't let the discussion go on so long that it becomes a useless digression from learning the subject you've been hired to teach and the students are expected to learn.

If these approaches don't work, use the authority of the school to re-establish order. First, warn a misbehaving individual, "If you can't settle down so that we can go on, I'll have to send you to the office," not, "The next person who says a word will be sent to the office," because sure as fate that next person will be a cooperative, orderly soul who is just trying to be helpful, and there you are with your threat hanging out.

Then, if misbehavior continues, do send the person from your room to a specific place, preferably with a note, and follow it up afterwards by talking with the student and with the staff member to whom the student was sent. It is very important not simply to send a student out of the room. Constructive action must follow to help develop behavior that works well for the student and the school.

Finally, don't feel weak or ashamed about using others in the school to help maintain order in your classroom, which, if you do it sooner rather than later, you will probably not have to do again, or at least not often.

Three contributions to order

A major contribution to good order is for you as a teacher always to act as an adult, not to try to be one of the kids. This doesn't mean setting up barriers, but just recognizing a proper order of society and chronology. Students have plenty of other students to talk to but relatively few mature teachers, so if you act your age, speak your age, and dress your age — and still are open and ready to listen and help — you are teaching your students to deal realistically with their world outside school.

Yet another sort of order you as teacher can help promote is the order of truthfulness. You can expect your students to be truthful, but don't be blind to the fact that they often are not — even if only to protect a friend. Never lie to a student. If you don't know the answer, say so; if you choose not to comment on a topic or situation, say so, but never make up an answer and never deceive.

Third, you can let your classroom exemplify a kind of order. It should be kept clean, even if you have to clean it yourself, but it is better if you can persuade the students to help. I always keep a can of scouring powder and some rags in the closet for cleaning desktops and walls. If students are around, I ask them to help. Before long, the amount of deliberate desk marking falls to near zero. After all, if I don't care enough to keep the place clean, why should the students?

Order and young children

It is perhaps even more important to establish a good base of order with very young children than with older ones. Most upper school teachers, seeing the easy, happy, seemingly casual behavior of a good nursery school or kindergarten, do not fully appreciate the planning, thought, care and expertise that have gone into making things run well and setting the stage for learning.

In some schools, the teacher visits the child at home before school opens, sees his or her room, and establishes the beginnings of a friendly relationship. Often, only half the group comes the first day, and the other half the second day, so that lots of individual attention can be given each child as he enters the school, begins to learn the system, and becomes willing to separate from the parent who accompanies him.

Procedures differ, but here is a typical one. Greet each child with a cheery welcome and take him to his (or her to her) own place — locker, cubby, table and chair — where he can put his things, which he can call his very own, and on which his name is written along with a picture of a rabbit, house, car, bird, hat, wheel, or whatever. Then hang a cardboard placard with his name and picture around his neck for all to see — *his* name. Give him a quick tour of the premises, especially the bathroom, and allow him to choose a quiet activity from the many available (blocks, crayons, scissors and paper, push toys) to keep himself busy until everyone has arrived.

Then give an attention signal — a chord on the piano, lights flashed off and on — and, once everybody is quiet, have the children assemble in a circle on the rug. Have each child say his name, which you repeat loudly and clearly. Invite each child to tell about anything he wants to (no one has to speak), perhaps starting off with you. Then you can go on to some other interesting, entertaining activity, such as a song, game, or story that everyone will like — even better than being at home.

After another free period, give the attention signal for juice time and its sensible routine: wash your hands, pick up your cup, pass by the pourer, sit down and drink at the tables anywhere you wish, get up and push your chair in when you've finished, drop your cup in the wastebasket, and go to the rug.

When nap time comes, excuse people to the nap mats, one or a few at a time (by name, or by categories — all with red socks, all with hair ribbons, all with belts), where they stay quietly, with a toy if they wish, and no obligation to go to sleep.

Since most nursery school and kindergarten children arrive with an attitude of awe rather than bumptiousness, the purpose of these routines, in the early days, is to establish a safe, consistent setting with reliable boundaries that make the children feel comfortable, free, happy, and stimulated: "This is *our* place."

As time goes on, an understanding of certain rules gradually develops: be kind, be helpful, share, take turns, what you take out put away when you're done with it, throw things in the wastebaskets, no pushing, no piling (unless it's a piling game), no running (except in the running place), no squashing, no shouting (unless it's a shouting game), no screaming indoors, no hitting (if you need to hit, go punch the punching balloon — a large plastic beanbag), no messing with other people's cubbies, and if you need help, ask for it.

Order and rules

When we think of order, most of us think of rules. In my experience, the best schools have the fewest rules. But students, at least bright ones in grades 4-10 or so, tend to like making up complicated systems of rules as a substitute for figuring out what to do about the various situations that arise.

Remember, however, that figuring out and discussing what to do about problems of human relations are just about the most important part of education. Having too many rules stifles this kind of thinking. The main things about rules are three: (1) they should be few, needed, and written down; (2) they should all be open for discussion and change; and (3) they should be obeyed until changed.

The rules given above for nursery school and kindergarten might be adapted to work for any grade. Here's a list for a typical well-run upper school.

1. Attend all classes and required activities and arrive on time.
2. Dress appropriately for the occasion and wear shoes.
3. Do not smoke, drink, or use drugs for nonmedical purposes.
4. Eat only in the lunchroom unless given permission to take lunch to a class or planned meeting.
5. Do not talk in places reserved for quiet study.
6. Do not run indoors.
7. Do not make loud noises indoors.
8. Do not take, borrow, or interfere with other people's belongings or school property.

9. Do not litter.
10. Do not leave the school grounds except with proper permission.

Some schools may need more rules, some fewer. Often rules are a sensible subject for discussion, for writing, for group thought. It is the professional duty of all teachers to know and enforce the rules of the school, even though they may not approve of some of them. The only exception is in a teacher's own classroom, where some important educational purpose might be served by not applying the rules (though I can't think why any teacher should need to permit exceptions to any of the ten rules just listed).

It is amazing how sensible youngsters can be when they have the legitimate task of working out rules and procedures for themselves. One example is the following manifesto, found posted on a clubhouse inhabited by eight-year-old boys. Neither the United Nations nor Congress has ever written a statement of greater scope, subtlety, and realism in relation to its purpose.

Club Rules (obay)

1. Be friends together
2. No sudden moves
3. Peaceful wars
4. Unpeaceful wars if necessary
5. No teasing at all
6. Gim practice every day
7. Help each other if nessasery
8. If running away do not chass

It is very easy to fall into the error of appreciating order for its own sake. To the simple-minded, education is merely a matter of telling children how to behave and punishing them when they don't fit the mold; of preaching what to believe and having them say, "We believe," or at least not hearing them object; and of filling their heretofore empty cranial stomachs with knowledge fed in by teachers that is returned — verbatim, unchewed, and undigested — onto a test paper, preferably in easily measured driblets.

In 1925, educator Agnes de Lima wrote *Our Enemy the Child* (New York: Arno Press), in which she castigates the ordermongers thus: "On one thing only are they agreed — the child . . . must be subdued and transformed from the alien, independent being he was created, to a creature more pliant to their purposes. The theory of infant damnation still animates too much of our educational policy. Children must be cured of their original sin, have the nonsense knocked out of them, be molded into shape, made fit for society."

A more recent teacher, Kim Marshall, in his excellent book *Law and Order in Grade 6-E* (Boston: Little, Brown, 1972), compares students in schools to "tidal pools near the ocean, in which a marvelous and colorful variety of marine life flourishes — crabs, underwater flowers, and so forth — when the water is calm. . . . The effect of the strict disciplinarian on kids [is] . . . similar to the effect of the incoming tides on these pools: the flowers close up tight, the crabs run into cracks and caves, and everything becomes still and colorless as the waves pound overhead."

2.
Interest

Hint 34. Don't waste time in the class having things explained that are well understood.
Abbie G. Hall

The best sort of order in school is not the order imposed from above or by a sense of duty. It is the order that results from interest in subjects being studied and the stimulation provided. I was struck by this a few years ago in a Quaker meeting for worship as I looked out over a sea of 250 children in grades 2-6. They were well-behaved and quiet but in a constant state of mild bodily writhing that reminded me of seaweed moving in the gentle currents of benign tropical waters.

Moved to rise and speak, I told a story about nearly falling off a mountain. As the suspense grew, the writhing ceased. Everyone gradually became motionless, intent on the story, until the suspense point passed (I didn't fall off the ledge). As I ended by drawing a brief lesson from the experience, the sea-weed again resumed its gentle movement. Thus interest creates order.

Further, truly good order is maintained by interest. In Chapters 5 and 6, I suggest some ways of teaching skills and subject matter that hold interest and result in good learning. For now, I will state a few general ideas.

● Make your classroom attractive and stimulating. The room should at least be clean and neat (but not sterile and prissily tidy) and as well provided as you can manage with posters, pictures, books, maps, games, and other physical tools of learning. The room should not be allowed to exemplify sloppiness, disrespect for property, or lack of care about appearance. Another possibility is an absolutely clean, bare room on the first day of school, with lots of empty space on walls, shelves, and surfaces to be decorated and filled. Students often rise delightedly to the challenge of decorating and enlivening their own room. However, the dull, bare room — especially a dirty, marked-up, dull, bare room — should not sit unimproved for more than a few days.

• Be convinced that the subjects and skills you teach are important to the lives, needs, and interests of your students. If you aren't, change what you are teaching or change jobs. Your own interest and conviction are contagious; so are your boredom and indecision.

• Allow for digressions. Don't be so obsessed with the essentialness of every lesson and class period that you can't give way to something very special and off the subject that may come up, like an all-day trip, or an unexpected, interesting visitor, or a burning concern that arises right in your class and causes a legitimate digression. In other words, be convinced of the importance of what you and the class are doing, but keep it in perspective.

• Be sure that everyone in the class has enough to do and gets some feeling of reward and satisfaction from doing it.

• Know, or learn as quickly as you can, your students' attention span and try not to exceed it. Quite normally, it will differ for each student from day to day, from subject to subject, and from activity to activity. If you observe carefully, you will come to know when it is force from outside rather than interest from within that is the main motivating force.

• Always be ready for a change of pace or activity if interest is flagging. It doesn't hurt to have a few games or contests in your repertoire, and even a joke or two. At times, I've been reduced to playing "Simon Says" or doing calisthenics, with no one the worse for it — and at least the blood gets moving.

Two kinds of motivation

Be aware that there are two kinds of motivation: inherent and extraneous. Inherent motivation, the better kind, arises from interest and pleasure in the subject itself or from the students' sense that the skills being taught are important to them. Extraneous motivation exists outside the matter being taught — the desire to be good, to stay out of trouble, to please the teacher, to do well on a test, to get good marks, or the pressure of parents or of peers.

It is unrealistic to expect that inherent, pure interest, pleasure, and importance of the tasks at hand will be a constant force. And this is not necessarily bad, for the strong desire to get a good mark, if realized, results in a solid sense of achievement and perhaps enough learning to make the next steps more naturally interesting. Working to please the teacher, normally a rather low form of motivation, is better than none. I can even remember times when I deliberately set out to get certain students to like me, and thus want to please me, simply to get them to learn something that they really needed to learn. The important thing here is not to allow this motivation to become so connected to you that when you are gone all motivation is gone with you and the student says, in effect, "Well, I learned math for Mrs. X because she's nice, but I sure won't do it for that old grouch Mr. Y." In general, if a very high proportion of motivation for learning is extraneous, the learning is less likely to last, and the motivation is more likely to shift to rebellion or to being turned off.

Relevance and interest

Try to teach, to show, to prove the relevance of everything your students are assigned or required to do. Explain, or get them to explain through discussion, why the stuff is worth learning. If you can't convince them that it's relevant, and they can convince you that it's irrelevant, stop teaching it until you can figure a better reason to do so.

By "relevance," I don't mean just something that will help students earn a living, even though that is legitimate. The eventual achievement of pleasure from Latin literature, after two years of suffering through grammar and Caesar, is relevant, if you can show it to be, but being able to read what it says on coins and knowing what *bis in die* means on a prescription is not. Meeting college requirements, getting on a varsity team, or being promoted to the next grade are relevant, if not the highest-grade, reasons for learning for those who want to achieve those objectives.

Be ingenious, persuasive, and constant in explaining the relevance of what you teach. And don't exaggerate.

3.
Spirit

Without order nothing much else is possible, but in the long run spirit is much more important than order. A good spirit in a school arises partly from interest — interested students can hardly help displaying a good spirit — and partly from the way you as a teacher treat the students and the way they treat one another. With good relations in the classroom, or in a class, almost any other good thing is possible.

Creating a good spirit

How do you create a good spirit? Let me suggest seven do's and seven don'ts, starting with the do's.

1. *Be kind.* Through observation, intelligence, and empathy, try to figure out what each student needs and, to the best of your ability, provide it.

2. *Be polite.* Even when others are not polite to you, be courteous and considerate in your behavior and language. Remember, politeness and firmness can go together.

3. *Be funny.* Recognize and enjoy funny things when they happen. Sometimes it's hard to keep enough perspective to see the humor, but it may come to you later, and then you can laugh with the class about it tomorrow. As James Thurber said, "Humor is emotional chaos remembered in tranquillity." If you and the class can't solve a problem, the next best thing is to find some humor in it. And don't be afraid to tell a joke or perform an antic.

4. *Laugh.* Be sure always to laugh *with* your students, or *at* a situation. Victor Borge, the comedian-pianist, has said, "The shortest distance between two people is a good laugh." Certainly, laughing together brings a group together, and the memory of laughing keeps it together.

5. *Let your students be funny.* Some teachers, fearful of losing control, try to make themselves the principal source of humor. This is needlessly timid. If any student can get a laugh from you and the class together, his feeling about himself and how he fits in improves, his spirits are raised, and spirit improves.

6. *Find something special, something that you admire, about each student.* Look hard, listen well, and find something, even if you have to write down the special thing you observe in order to remember it. And be sure to find a chance to remark on it in public or private, whichever seems appropriate.

7. *Respect each student.* Regardless of what happens or who does or says what, never forget that each individual in each class has infinite worth and potential. If you respect and show your respect for every student, each one will be more likely to respect himself. The students who seem least lovable to you probably are difficult for others to love, too, so they are most greatly in need of your expressions and actions of affection and respect. Obviously, you can't and shouldn't respect all kinds of action and behavior, but the *person* who acts and behaves, no matter how badly, must have your respect.

Now the don'ts for helping to create a good spirit.

1. *Don't get angry at a person or a class.* If you must get angry, try to be angry at a situation or an action, for anger toward a person is likely to beget more anger, close off communication, and ruin spirit. If you do get angry, have the grace to apologize, which you can do without excusing the inexcusable behavior that may have angered you.

2. *Don't scold.* Scolding finds fault and poisons spirit. It is an immoral luxury enjoyed by small people in authority.

3. *Don't be cruel.* There is no excuse for inflicting pain and hardship for its own sake — which cruelty does — and even less for enjoying it.

4. *Don't embarrass students and make them uncomfortably self conscious.* It rarely helps for a teacher to point out a student's faults, even though he may have faults and behave in

harmful ways, and never in public. Later in this chapter and in the next one, I have some suggestions for how to deal with faults and poor behavior.

5. *Don't use sarcasm.* Wit is fine and humor a blessing, but sarcasm — wit used to show scorn or contempt — is just another form of cruelty, and it's even worse than cynicism.

6. *Don't make jokes about a person's name.* Even if a joke is OK and doesn't offend the person who has the name, chances are that he has heard the joke dozens of times. On the other hand, a child may be pleased if you invent a friendly nickname, but even that might not go over. It's best, by and large, to play it straight with people's names.

7. *Don't invade a student's privacy.* Students may reveal many private things about themselves in the course of a discussion, just as you as a teacher may reveal parts of your private life. What makes these intimate exchanges acceptable, in a private conversation or in a class discussion, is that they are voluntary. But if a teacher even gives the appearance of prying or snooping, the spirit is spoiled and the barriers go up.

Class meetings and good spirit

Kim Marshall says, in *Law and Order in Grade 6-E* (Boston: Little, Brown, 1972), that "most kids are not about to be remade." Most have basic self-respect, and they don't want anyone trying to change the basic self that they respect.

Most classes are not about to be remade, either. They can remake themselves, and they can be helped in the process, but it is rare that a teacher can say, "Be and act this way," and get the class to do it. The success of individuals and of groups is that they feel they control their own destiny and that they figure out their own ways to improve their spirit and behavior. Later on, I will offer suggestions for giving individual students a sense of control over their academic destiny. Here, let me suggest how they can be helped to achieve a degree of control over the spirit and destiny of their classroom group (or any other defined group in school).

The way is through class meetings. Using class meetings to help groups solve social problems and improve their welfare and success as a group has been done by thousands of teachers over the years. This technique is especially well explained and given a good theoretical basis by psychiatrist William Glasser in *Schools without Failure* (New York: Harper & Row, 1969), a well-written, short, interesting book based on his experiences in crowded urban public schools. Every teacher should read it.

Some of the kinds of problems that can be worked on in class meetings are fighting, bad language, unfriendliness, bullying, making a mess in the cafeteria, rushing to lunch tables and shutting out unpopular people, not helping people who are lonely and friendless, bossy people, destruction of property, truancy, noise and pushing in the halls, forms of cruelty and persecution like teasing or hiding book bags, stealing or messing with other people's property, not getting homework done, not settling down at the start of class, a feeling that schoolwork is dull and pointless, cheating and copying other people's work, feeling too tightly (or not tightly enough) controlled by the teacher, not having enough fun in school, not taking turns with scarce equipment, a feeling that the teacher has pets, objecting to other people because they are dirty or smelly, and treating others badly because of their race.

Almost any class or school group will exhibit some of these kinds of behavior or feelings from time to time, and they are bound to have a bad effect on group spirit if they are not dealt with. The all too typical way for a teacher to try to deal with them is to tell — to tell the class what he or she thinks the problem is, sometimes objectively, sometimes in a voice tinged with blame, to tell the class how it should behave and how much nicer things would be if it did, to tell what the consequences will be (for the group or for individuals) if people don't behave properly.

In a group that is strongly motivated by family and other forces outside the school, this teacher-preacher-punisher system may work, at least for a time. It's how most of us were treated, and it has the advantage of being simple, obvious, and easy to apply. But in most situations, especially those where the problem is serious and the spirit not so good, it doesn't work at all, or not for very long.

Why? Because it doesn't involve any thinking or observing, only listening and possibly obeying; it doesn't make anyone figure out solutions; it doesn't ask anything of the class except to avoid punishment by behaving in a teacher-prescribed way; and it may encourage students to evade or deny problems or to try to lie their way out of responsibility for behavior that doesn't work.

The class meeting method works quite differently. The class is called into discussion as a working group to solve problems by an exchange of ideas and by a good deal of brainwork. Class meeting discussions usually work best if the group moves into a tight circle (including the teacher), where it is easy for everyone to hear and see everyone else. The steps in the process are these.

1. *The class exposes the problem.* The teacher may start by posing a question: "I hear a lot of people complaining that there's too much messing around with other people's things. Is this just a lot of talk, or is there really a problem?" The teacher then presides over a discussion designed to bring out the facts. What is happening? Who is responsible? Is it widespread? Who's suffering? Any evidence is acceptable. If something is said that seems untrue — "Mary and Joe are always messing in people's desks, and they take money" — the group is asked, "Is that true?" Although Mary and Joe have a chance to deny it, they at least become aware that people think they are part of the problem and start to think about what they must do, or stop doing, to change how people think about them. Others may point out that it's not just Mary and Joe, or that property has been messed with when Mary and Joe weren't even around. It is always best to guide discussion toward reporting the facts rather than placing blame. The teacher should never blame and never judge. The teacher is there only to moderate and guide the discussion and try to get the facts out. If the discussion becomes too harsh and blame-oriented, the teacher can say, "Well, I see that there is a problem," and then have the class establish that a problem does exist and is serious enough to discuss some more.

2. *The class shows why the problem is bad for the group.* This phase may flow quite naturally from the discussion, or the teacher may start it by saying, "Let's move on and talk about whether the problem is really serious." Again, it is best to try to keep the emphasis off blame and to concentrate instead on how individuals and the group are being affected by the problem. Is it really harmful, or is it just people's imagination?

3. *The class tries to figure out or devise solutions to the*

problem. The teacher attempts to help the class figure out suggestions for better ways of behaving that will solve the problem. It's sometimes good to write practical suggestions on the board. It is essential in this phase that the solutions suggested be positive and not involve blame or punishment. In fact, this can be made a rule: "Let's talk only about what we can do to solve the problem." Unacceptable solutions involving blame and punishment for Joe and Mary, for instance, should be described for what they are: "That's just blaming and picking on two people." The teacher should then ask, "What things can we do, how can we behave, so that people's property will be safe?" Constructive suggestions, like buying locks for the desks, or having a public supply of materials that everyone can sign for and use, or everyone being readier to share or ask permission, can be induced by having the teacher make the first few.

4. *The class commits itself to trying the agreed-upon solutions.* Up to this point, the class has been involved in the educational process of thinking about its problems and figuring out solutions. This leads to habits of problem solving, develops communications skills, and turns people's energies toward acting better and not just retreating into disgust, dislike, hopelessness, and blaming. Now the meeting turns toward getting people to commit themselves to the better ways of behaving by stating openly that they'll try, by agreeing to take certain (write them down!) practical steps, or by signing a paper promising to try to behave in certain ways.

We all know that problems don't simply arise, get discussed, and get solved by people committing themselves to solutions. Identifying and solving problems is a constant process, and class meetings are a constantly useful part of the process. As one student, better at epigram than history, said, "Rome wasn't burnt in a day." But class meetings can keep students thinking about major problems and working to deal with them constructively. They develop the self-esteem, free communication, and sense of shared worthwhile objectives that foster a good spirit.

In Chapter 6, I give more specific suggestions for ways to conduct a good classroom discussion. First, however, let's look at a subject that is closely allied to order, interest, and spirit: discipline.

4.
Discipline

Hint 54. Discipline should aim at improving
the character.   *Abbie G. Hall*

Although "discipline" derives from the Latin *discere*, "to
learn," in the minds of many people it has become synony-
mous with order and punishment. People seem to think that
one of the worst things you can say about a teacher is that he or
she is "not a good disciplinarian," and the greatest concern
about our schools is "lack of discipline." This means, I gather,
disorderliness and bad behavior, which people believe result
from the failure of schools to be strict, to make demands, and,
when trouble breaks out, to punish. Of course, almost anyone
who has ever taught school knows that things aren't nearly as
simple as that.

One definition of discipline, according to the *Standard College Dictionary*, is "systematic training in obedience to rules
and authority, as in the armed forces." Such discipline may
work in some schools, and, during brief moments, in individual classrooms, but in the long run, as a steady school diet,
such imposed discipline is not congenial to learning and does
not develop character or maturity.

A second definition of discipline, from the same dictionary,
is "training of the mental, moral, and physical powers by instruction, control, and exercise." Now that's a good, broad,
acceptable definition for us teachers, especially if we are competent in our instruction, if we are able to arrange things so
that the forces of "control" shift from outside the student to
inside, and if we provide plenty of opportunity for the "exercise" — the use — of the student's powers.

Developing self-discipline

We will never know whether our students have developed any inner discipline, self-control, or independent motivation unless we remove external controls and see what happens. One powerful element of external control is our conspicuous watching. Don't get me wrong: students need to be watched, and teachers who have developed, like P. G. Wodehouse's character Aunt Dahlia, "an eye that could open an oyster at twenty paces," possess a useful tool, much more effective and less distracting to others than a yell or a snarl.

Speaking of watching, I know a high school teacher, Emma, a tough, gentle, experienced professional, who told me that she had become expert in what she called the "overhead-backhand" method of writing. It enabled her to write on the board without ever taking her eye off the class. "It takes practice," Emma said, "but it is very useful. In schools like mine, to face away from the class for even a moment can mean disruption, ridicule, humiliation, and even personal injury" — a distorted Golden Rule applied: "Do unto others before they do unto you."

We must, however, be careful not to rely too much on the overhead-backhand technique, for an overwatched class never learns self-discipline. The key to helping students develop self-discipline, at least in a large, fairly traditional school, is to give them as much freedom to control and motivate themselves as they can use, and occasionally a little bit more. This means that we start with order and control, then put them on their own, bit by bit.

We measure out careful doses, starting by allowing the class to work independently on well-defined tasks while we work with individuals or small groups. We then encourage the class to devise routines for settling down and getting to work at the start of the period (or, easier, at the end) while we sit in the back. As a next step, we leave the class alone unexpectedly for a few minutes, arriving late on purpose in order to see what happens. Finally, we let individuals or small groups go to the library or work independently in the hall or in another room while we stay with the rest of the class.

Those are only a few examples of allowed opportunities for

students to "control and exercise" their "mental, moral, and physical powers" independent of our presence. In fact, in many an excellent open classroom students of all ages spend large portions of the day in self-controlled educational exercise of their powers.

The saying "We fail toward success" is often true of developing discipline in school. If we occasionally grant individual students or a class more freedom than they can manage successfully, temporary failure will result and discipline will break down. The breakdown of self-discipline can be the occasion for some excellent learning, provided the occasion is not used for preaching and punishing at the same time. By meeting, exposing the problem, figuring out ways to do better next time, and then having the members of the class commit themselves to trying better ways, self-discipline is strengthened.

On the other hand, it is harmful for students (or anyone else) to be faced too often with challenges they are unable to meet. Teachers and students can learn the extent of their joint capacity to succeed. As someone has said, "Courage is the memory of past successes"; so are self-respect and self-discipline.

Discipline and "talking to" students

I have suggested that we try in every way possible to build self-respect and feelings of self-control in each of our students. Too many experiences in school end up with students feeling that they, as individuals, are failures. We tend to criticize and hold up and preach standards that our students are not yet able to meet, then we correct and scold until they, feeling belittled, attacked, and devastated, become angry or withdraw and allow their emotions, not their brains, to direct their behavior.

I remember years ago seeing a drawing of two girls relaxing and confiding, with one saying to the other, "You know, the trouble with me is that I'm the sort of person my mother doesn't want me to associate with." It's funny, but it's tragic. An eight-year-old schoolboy in Rochester, New York, revealed the same sort of discouragement in his essay on "What My Dog Means to Me." He wrote, "My dog means somebody nice and quiet to be with. He does not say, 'Do,' like my mother, or 'Don't,' like my father, or 'Stop,' like my big brother. My dog

Spot and I just sit together quietly and I like him and he likes me.''

We must support and respect our students, especially as individuals, as much as we can. That is quite different from supporting and respecting all their behavior. In my school, a teacher asked Herb, a seventh grader, to be quiet in a study period. Instead, Herb ran out of the room and down the hall with the teacher chasing him. As he zipped into another roomful of students quietly reading, the teacher caught him by the arm. After a dramatic silence, Herb shouted, ''Help! Help! Reality's got me by the arm!'' Reality then took him to a quiet place, and they talked over his behavior, but not his worth as a person, which, obviously, both he and the teacher respected.

One of the main opportunities we have to help students develop self-discipline and successful behavior is in our talks alone with them. What I am about to suggest is sensible, not very difficult, and it usually works. Some teachers have trouble with it because it goes contrary to their habits and to the way they remember being treated — scold-preach-punish, with the teacher doing most of the thinking and talking and the student mostly listening, resenting, and feeling put down.

The method works best in a private quiet session with the student, but it can also be used — briefly — right in a class when someone's behavior makes it necessary. It also works for guidance counselors and principals, and even for those poor souls called ''disciplinarians''; students who are sent to the principal or other higher authority come back from the session feeling better about themselves and behaving better.

The essential attitude the teacher and student must maintain, when following this method, is that the student's behavior, not the student as a person, is the problem. Always focus on the behavior and how it can be changed. Keep the atmosphere warm and friendly and objective. Now for the specific steps.

1. *Ask, do not tell, the student what he is (or was) doing.* If you are warm and friendly, he (or she) will tell you honestly, because you both know that help, not punishment, is your reason for talking together.

2. *Ask the student to decide whether his behavior is good or bad, helping or hindering.* Is it helping him, his classmates, the

school? Or, like Herb's disruption of study period, bad because it bothers others? (Being a confident, bright, and argumentative kid, Herb would probably also say that he *likes* to talk, that it really doesn't bother anyone, that he doesn't mind when other people talk, and that study periods are stupid, anyway. If he says this, you need to question him more deeply, especially about the effect of his behavior on himself, on others. Remember, you don't tell him; you ask him, and he thinks it out and tells you — himself.) This kind of questioning provides important education in responsibility, or acting out of knowledge of the consequences of what you do, both for yourself and for others, now and later. A class can profitably discuss various actions and their consequences.

3. *Ask the student to figure out a better way of behaving,* one that will work better for himself and for everyone else. (If, like Herb, the student has behaved this way for the twenty-sixth time, clearly the discussion needs to go deeper. If the student can't think of anything, you can help by making suggestions, in the form of questions: "Does where you sit have anything to do with the problem?" "Do you have any work or reading to do during study periods?"

4. *Ask the student to commit himself to a better way of behaving,* even to the point of writing a statement of intention to do or stop doing what's needed. Stating an intention is better than making a promise, because promises should not be broken, and you may feel you are bad or immoral if you don't keep a promise. An intention is only that — determination to do something, but without the moral overtones of a promise. If you don't have the strength or will to carry out an intention, you don't need to feel that you are a moral failure, or no good as a person, but only that you haven't been able to do what you honestly intended to do.

5. *Allow the consequences, good or bad, to happen. Accept no excuses if the student does not carry out his commitment.* This is very important. Too many of us teachers are too busy, too indulgent, or too hopeful that if we let something pass just this once it won't happen again. Students should not be protected from the reasonable consequences of their failing behavior. If the student fails, start again with step 1 until understanding, determination, and strength are developed. In

Schools without Failure (New York: Harper & Row, 1969), William Glasser says, "Teachers who care accept no excuses." He also says,

> Assuming that we learn to work with children by becoming personally involved and dealing with their present behavior, we must help them to change their behavior toward more success. To help a presently failing child to succeed, *we must get him to make a value judgment about what he is now doing that is contributing to his failure.* If he doesn't believe that what he is doing is contributing to his failure, if he believes his behavior is all right, no one can change the child now. He must then suffer the consequences of his refusal to change his behavior. *Neither school nor therapist should attempt to manipulate the world so that the child does not suffer the reasonable consequences of his behavior.* But we should not give up; accepting failure is not a reasonable consequence. No matter how often he fails, he should again and again be asked for a value judgment until he begins to doubt that what he is defending is really the best for him.

There are a number of don'ts connected with Glasser's method.

1. *Don't use a student's past against him.* It is helpful, of course, for you to be aware of the past (for example, that the student has displayed the same sort of failing behavior for several years) because almost certainly the student is also aware of it and feels weighed down by it. But never say anything like, "You've been acting this way ever since fourth grade. Aren't you ever going to stop?" That just generates a feeling of greater hopelessness. Instead, assume that right now is a new moment that offers a new beginning and a new chance for success.

2. *Don't preach or dictate.* That stops the student's brain-work; the point is to get him to figure out how to behave.

3. *Don't reject the student.* No matter what, stay friendly and objective. You're not out to remake the person; you're there to help him to behave successfully.

4. *Don't accept excuses.*

This method is even more appropriate for serious kinds of failing behavior, such as stealing, cheating, not doing one's work, antagonizing other students or teachers, habitual fighting, refusing to answer in class, cutting classes, using drugs or alcohol in school, coming to school dirty and smelly, rudely cutting down other people, and so on.

Discipline and punishment

I want to say a word about punishment, for punishment is our traditional response to someone's bad behavior: tell him it's bad, tell him to stop, and punish him for being bad.

I am always humbled, though, by a little survey in which some students (I think about nine or ten years old) were asked which they would prefer if they misbehaved — a spanking or a friendly talk with the teacher. They voted overwhelmingly for the spanking.

I can only suppose that they'd had "friendly talks" before and knew that such talks took a long time, were boring, covered what was obvious, required sitting still and listening, made you feel guilty and bad afterwards. Spankings, on the other hand, had the advantages of being short, being clean, making you feel you'd paid your debt, gotten what you deserved, and free to go out and be yourself again, with few regrets.

In my survey of the 400 middle schoolers, however, when I asked, "Has anyone at home or school, grades five through nine, ever used corporal punishment (spanking, hitting) on you?" 46 per cent of the boys said yes, 54 per cent no, and with the girls it was 40 per cent yes and 60 per cent no. In response to "What were the effects on you?" 29 per cent said that in one way or another they were good, 70 per cent bad.

Comments in favor of corporal punishment: "Corporal punishment keeps me from doing it again." "It's better because it was faster," "It makes me respect a person very close to me, and I'm glad it happened," "At home I've been spanked several times; I think this method really helps get the message across," and "I think it is more torturous to talk it out."

Here's what the opponents of corporal punishment said: "It does not make as big an impression on me as talking," "I felt bad," "Parents shouldn't hit their children unless they are little and they can't discuss it with them," "It made me a sad child," "It only hurts and builds grudges," "It does not explain what I did wrong or why," and "I get madder and go out of the way to do bad things."

Two comments I enjoyed were from seventh graders: "The effect was a soar rear [depicted]," and "My mother and father both think it is a hiteous idea." Another two comments were from eighth-grade girls: "My father and mother hit me up until 6th grade, when they devised other ingenious ways of making me behave," and "My mother hit me on the head with a frozen hot dog and I cried and screamed." A ninth-grade boy reported, "A certain Mr. X used to beat us with a piece of cypress that was conveniently shaped in the size of one's gluteus maximous (ass)."

Since nearly three quarters of the students said that the effects of corporal punishment were bad, I think we must give most weight to the comments that it makes the person "sad" (and probably angry), builds grudges, and doesn't give any insight into what the person did wrong or how he might do better next time. It is likely to lead to lying or to denial of the poor behavior.

In the case of the talkative, confident Herb, one might ask, "Doesn't this kid know perfectly well what's wrong with his behavior? Doesn't he get a bang out of all the attention it brings him? Aren't there shorter ways of dealing with him and leaving more time for really serious matters?" Yes, of course; launching Aunt Dahlia's oyster-opening glance or applying clean, no-nonsense punishment might do the trick. But if you are going to punish, I make the following suggestions.

● Never punish a failing child or student, only a basically confident, successful one who can take it in stride.

● Never use a punishment that humiliates, like forcing a child to write or say that you were right and he was wrong, or any kind of public punishment (except for a brief, factual, businesslike calldown, and even these can become bad habits for teachers.)

● Never withhold your love and appreciation for the child, and never attack him as a person.

● Let the punishment fit the crime, and, if possible, follow naturally from it. For example, logical punishment for cheating on a test is a no-credit mark, being assigned to study the material again, and being required to take another test. Relevant punishment for repeated talking in a quiet study period might be to sit at a desk away from everyone else. For littering, it could be having to pick up a bag of scraps in the hall or outdoors and bring them in for inspection.

• Consult with the student and let him suggest his own punishment. If it is fair, appropriate, and reasonable, use it.

• Never punish a student by requiring him to do more of something that is a vital part of his education, like writing an extra report, reading an extra book, or doing five more math problems. All that this does is to create or strengthen an association between legitimate work and bad feelings.

• Don't use silly punishments, like writing "I will never . . . again" 100 times, unless you and the culprit have a tacit, friendly understanding that "we're doing this because we have to do something."

Dealing with cheating

A special problem related to discipline and developing successful independence and self-respect is cheating. I think the commonly used automatic sequence of cheat-and-get-punished (if-you're-found-out) should be re-examined by all teachers who use it.

There's no question that cheating is fairly common in schools where conditions permit it and where there is any degree of competition or pressure. Some people argue that a good way to end cheating is to take the academic pressure off students and to give up marks. These steps would radically reduce cheating; after all, why cheat if there's no pressure and no marks? But eliminating pressure and marks does not teach honesty; it merely removes the motivation to cheat in school. The real challenge for schools is to teach honesty even when good performance is very important and when a reasonable amount of competition is present — two familiar parts of many segments of life.

When I asked the 400 students in grades 5-9 why they cheated (the cheating rate increased from 31 to 67 per cent from grade 5 to grade 9), they gave these reasons, arranged in descending order of frequency: "I want a good grade," "I forgot to study," "To get the answer," "It's a game, and when the person's not looking it's their fault," "When the answers are right under your nose and the problem is much too hard," "Everybody was doing it," "I'm scared if I flunk my parents will punish me," and "When I know how to do it and it gets boring."

Common sense, experience, and the replies quoted above show that cheating is likely to take place when one or more of the following conditions are present: seats are too close together, the teacher is not alert, and test answers are easy to spot; the work tested or assigned seems pointless or unreasonable; the work is hard and not well taught; there is tremendous emphasis on marks for their own sake; and students strongly dislike or do not respect the teacher.

Let me suggest some policies and practices that work well to decrease cheating.

• Try to keep the work interesting and convince the students that it's important to learn it. Make it challenging but never beyond the capacity of most of the class.

• Admit frankly before the first test of the year that cheating often occurs in school and say that it's only sensible to move desks apart and cover answers that are easy to see. Without making students feel any distrust on your part, you will convey the idea that you know what's what.

• Find an early opportunity for class discussion of reasons for cheating and its effects. It's surprising how many students have never thought much about it.

• Keep alert during tests (this doesn't mean a constant glare), and, when marking papers, watch for verbatim similarities. Don't be blindly trusting.

• Quietly take away the paper of any student who is clearly cheating, give no credit for the test, and confer inconspicuously after class to arrange a time to talk privately. "Setting an example" by drastic, overt action is not only unnecessary but often creates such bitterness and alarm that no lessons in honesty can be taught.

• When you talk privately, find out from the student why he (or she) cheated and try to help him overcome the need for it. Get him to explain, if he can, how cheating is self-defeating and how it may affect his reputation. But you must also explain that cheating is quite frequent and that this particular episode, while serious, does not put a permanent blot on his record, especially if he doesn't cheat again.

• Ask the student whether he would like to have you tell his parents what happened or whether he'd rather do it himself. Explain that parents should know when their child is in trouble so that they can help. If a child is obviously afraid of his parents (and a surprising number of those who cheat are), you might let him off this time without telling his parents. If he says he will talk to them, then ask him in a day or two how they reacted.

No teachers — or parents, when they know about it — should let an incident of cheating or other dishonesty pass undealt with. If people get away with cheating (or stealing, or lying), they're more likely to keep on doing it. In the long run, dealing promptly and definitely with cheating and taking enough time to do it will help to prevent future incidents. More important, it will save the morale of the offender and the others involved. Honesty does not grow naturally; it is nurtured as teachers, students, and parents speak and act in situations where honesty is tested.

In schools where the students are encouraged to work together in order to teach one another, it is important to teach children in the early grades that there are certain special times — when you take tests — when you have to work alone and when sharing ideas and information is not permitted. Be sure that they understand, through discussion, the reasons for tests and the special way people have to behave during them.

The influence of a teacher's example

To the earlier definition of discipline as "training the mental, moral, and physical powers by instruction, control and exercise" I should add one other means of developing discipline: your example. It's tiresome, I know, to be told that you have to exemplify all the qualities that you are expected to teach. But the better example you set, the better your teaching of self-discipline will be. I suggest six qualities that all of us as teachers need to keep in mind.

1. *Reliability.* Let your yea be yea and your nay nay unless

you are shown to be wrong, in which case admit it; don't hide it.

2. *Honesty.* Never lie or distort, if you can help it. Be honest about your errors, and your students will be honest about theirs.

3. *Promptness.* It takes no longer to read and mark homework and papers today than it will next week. If you know you can't get papers back promptly, say so and tell why. Otherwise, be just as punctual as you expect your students to be.

4. *Sensitivity.* Show that you are aware of how your class is feeling as a group and as individuals. Chapter 24, "Keeping in Touch," gives some suggestions on how to go about this.

5. *Self-control.* Show that you are in control of your powers — especially your power of language, which is usually superior to that of your students — and use them responsibly. This doesn't mean being a prissy, teachery talker, but a considerate one. And when the occasion arises, try to demonstrate how to control feelings by frankly telling the class how certain kinds of behavior make you feel rather than by letting yourself be carried away by those feelings.

6. *Fairness.* There is practically nothing students resent more than unfairness or the appearance of unfairness. Never have a pet, or if you do have one — some students are certainly easier than others to like or enjoy — keep it a secret. Sometimes, of course, there are good reasons for treating one student differently from another in the same circumstances, but the reasons should not be based on favoritism. It's healthy practice to tell classes you believe in fairness and are going to do your best to be fair but to admit that you aren't perfect and may slip unintentionally from time to time. Ask your students to tell you when they think you are being unfair so that you can either correct the injustice or explain why you did what you did.

Be sure, as you try to exemplify these qualities, that you do not seem to be saying, by your demeanor, "Look at me! How good I am!" Just *be*, the best you can, and remember the little child's prayer: "Dear God, please make the bad people good and the good people nice."

5.
Learning the Basics: Instruction

Hint 11. Every thing that is explained to a pupil which he can find out for himself robs him of so much education.   *Abbie G. Hall*

Having talked about the conditions necessary for good learning, now what about learning itself? How do children learn? How do we encourage students to learn what they need to learn in order to lead useful, happy, satisfying lives?

First, we need to dispel the widely held false notion that teaching is the same thing as learning. It is not, as suggested by James R. Newman, in *The World of Mathematics* (New York: Simon & Schuster, 1956): "There are two ways to teach mathematics. One is to take real pains toward creating understanding. . . . The other is the old British system of teaching until you're blue in the face."

We can all think back to times when a teacher was putting on a good verbal and physical show but no learning was taking place. Let's face it: most of the learning that occurs in our classrooms occurs not because of direct oral instruction but because of conditions we help to create that cause students to learn for themselves and from one another. Now and then, the right utterance at the right moment may cause a sudden surge of understanding, but not very often. Most of what we say *at* our students, mostly from the front of the room, may look fine to a passing supervisor, and it may even impress the students as being exactly what a teacher is supposed to do, but let's not fool ourselves.

The acid test for a school is whether it succeeds in teaching the basics, especially the ones it is supposed to teach, which are, I suppose, reading, writing, and arithmetic. If your school doesn't teach kids to read and write and figure to the best of their ability, and if it cannot show by objective measures that it is doing so, it might as well go out of business, no matter how many other fine and noble things it is doing, or claims to be doing. The trouble with such a crude, trite statement, however, is that it encourages simplistic, uninformed people to think that in order to teach the 3 R's you just put kids in rooms with rows and *teach,* either by pouring or hammering in, and when you're tired of doing that you get out the workbooks.

What are the basics?

Before talking here about instruction, and, later, discussion, I must first set forth a somewhat more complete and useful statement of what the basics are than the one given above. I have found it helpful to divide them into three categories: basic skills, basic substance, and basic attitudes, with "basic" meaning "necessary to know in order to lead a useful, happy, satisfying life in our society, today and tomorrow."

Here's my list. Yours may differ somewhat, and so may mine a year from now, but probably not much. Similarly, my ideas of which basics are teachable primarily through instruction and which ones through discussion may differ from yours, but not to any significant degree.

1. *Basic skills* — to speak, to listen and hear, to see and observe, to exchange (communicate), to read, to write, to figure and compute (arithmetic), to think logically, to organize, to persuade, to deal with conflict, to deal with "the media," to judge when to try to solve a problem and when to try to live with it.

2. *Basic substance* — to know how the world and the universe work (the sciences, nature study, mathematics, geography); to know how humankind works — in individuals and in my own culture, and in other cultures (psychology, anthropology, sociology); to know what humankind has done and thought (history); to be aware of what the important questions are ("What does what I am studying mean?" "What still needs to be discovered? By me? By humankind?").

3. *Basic attitudes* — to be interested and curious, to be per-

suadable, to respect myself, to respect others (which requires imagination, the ability to project myself into the situation of others), to respect knowledge, to feel a tension between what is and what should be, to feel responsible for my actions (which requires the skill of foreseeing and evaluating consequences).

I suggest that you measure against these basics everything you and your students do.

Instruction

Instruction and discussion should rarely be separated in school, and I only separate them here for simplicity's sake. (See Chapter 6, which deals with discussion.) Even the sort of instruction that comes from reading an assignment should involve constant mental discussion with the book as readers try to master its content.

Out and out instruction does have its place, however. When a student or a group really wants to know an answer and needs it now, and when there is an answer and the teacher has it, often it is best to say, "OK, I'll explain," or "Here, let me show you," and to go ahead and explain or show. But if the main value to the students will come from thinking out the answer or figuring out for themselves what to do, or if it will come not from asking the teacher but asking the class, then it is best for the teacher not to instruct or give an answer. Teaching is not answering; it is asking questions and providing the means to find answers. And most of the questions should not be the sort that can be answered yes or no.

Of course, teachers shouldn't merely preside over exchanges of ignorance. That's an even greater waste of time than giving too many answers. When misstatements of fact are made, they should be corrected, and when no one knows the facts, they should be found out, preferably by a student. Sometimes a few minutes of organized information giving are called for, when interest is high and facts are needed in order to continue the discussion.

For example, if someone writes on the board, "Haveing eaten our lunch, the car wouldn't start," it's usually better to have the class examine the sentence, discover the errors, and correct them than for the teacher simply to fix them or call on the first person who shouts out. If in the process some further understanding can be developed about rules (generalizations that are true), so much the better. But if somebody says, "You don't need an apostrophe to understand 'wouldnt,' " that's not an error for correction; it's a conviction worth discussing, requiring the class to weigh the values of simple "correctness" as a social grace versus the apostrophe as a bother and abomination that is almost never really needed.

The class may discover that the truth, or understanding, is not something to be crammed into us but to be drawn out of us. The best teachers create and capitalize on opportunities to involve their classes in discussion of the philosophical and moral aspects of whatever subjects are being studied.

Like most teachers, I am strongly biased toward books and reading as sources of instruction. Books, I feel, are the very best teaching machines: they are simple to operate, easy to program to meet individual needs; they don't burn out or break when dropped or come unplugged; and they're comparatively cheap.

However, we bookish teachers, so good at reading, must remember that some — and sometimes most — of our students aren't very good at books and reading but still are well able to learn. For them, good instruction may be by brief oral presentation, panel discussion, film, drawing, arguing, touching and handling, trying it out in the lab, taking a trip or walk, or having to explain it to somebody else.

Instruction, then, should be many-dimensional and involve more than one sense. That's why every classroom should have plenty of blackboard space, chalk, and erasers. Then, when a new word comes up, it can be written on the board to be seen as well as heard without interrupting whatever else is going on. Chapter 13 contains some specific suggestions for various kinds of nonbook instruction.

Instruction and sequence

In giving instruction in most classrooms and in most subjects, we must give attention to the sequence in which we present the elements of the material. We make many mistakes because we try to teach a skill or concept before the students know another one they need first in order to understand.

For instance, you can't learn to multiply until you know how to add, to do algebra before arithmetic; you can't really observe the behavior of a snake or a mouse until you are free of fascination and fear, or understand why the stars don't fall down unless you know a lot of other things first. Most important, you can't learn much of anything academic unless you know how to read — even though bright dyslectics can fool the teacher and themselves by guessing their way and piecing together oral and printed clues, not really reading.

A word of caution, however. The sequence concept does not apply to and should not be forced upon certain important areas of learning. For example, it is not true that you can't read until you can say, "Kuh, aah, tuh — cat," or write a sentence until you know the parts of speech, or a paragraph until you know a sentence. Many crimes against learning are committed by forcing children who can write fluently to stop and go back to attacking the language piecemeal. The same holds true with drawing and painting and repairing your bike.

Teachers need to figure out and keep figuring out what students need to learn before they can learn something else. They need to avoid the utter waste of trying to teach multiplication before addition or of making kids learn to stay inside the lines while coloring before being allowed to express themselves in art.

Developmental sequence: thinking

Another kind of sequence has to do with whether or not a student has developed the ability to do abstract thinking. For years, teachers have been aware simply from common-sense observation that some students can think abstractly and some cannot.

Swiss psychologist Jean Piaget, a brilliant observer of children's thought processes, especially their ability to think logically, notes that "intelligence," whatever that may be, does not increase at a steady rate but in spurts. Thus, the conventional IQ score, based on a performance-age ratio, often is not an accurate measure of intelligence because people shift from one stage of thinking to a higher stage at different ages. Piaget also observes that children and young people develop their capacity for logical thinking quite independently of their emotional surroundings.

Piaget has outlined four stages of development, the first of which he calls the *sensorimotor period*, when the child perceives the world directly through the physical senses. By about age two, the child has learned that actions have physical consequences and that he and his environment are not one and the same.

The second stage, the *period of prelogical thought*, typically lasts from age two to age five. The child's thinking during this stage contains a sort of "magical" element, wherein the child is unable to distinguish clearly between events and objects that are experienced and those that are imagined. Many children are still in this stage in nursery school and kindergarten.

During the third stage, the *period of concrete operations*, the child learns to observe, count, organize, remember, and reorganize concrete objects and to do mental operations without losing the distinction between real and imaginary. This stage lasts until about age eleven or twelve, *if* the child involved is going to move on to the fourth stage of development of thought. Many people never do.

When those who go on do enter the fourth stage, the *period of formal operations*, they begin to be able to deal with abstractions, to reason about the future, to understand and construct systems of thought, and to put forth theories and test them. This stage comes with adolescence, typically between the ages of eleven and fifteen or sixteen, though it may come much later (and, in a few people, earlier). But nearly half of all Americans never reach "adolescence" in their capacity to think. That is, they never learn to think abstractly, never reach the stage where they re-examine their world or the people in it or themselves. It is important for teachers to know this, because to require a person who has not reached the period of formal operations to think abstractly is to require the impossible.

As far as I know, we have no simple test to show whether or not a student has reached the formal operations stage. I would guess, however, that a student who has reached sixth grade and has an IQ score around 120 would be able to think abstractly, and that one in ninth grade with a score around 115 could also do so. These are only guesses, though, and you should check them against your own observation of what students say and write.

An instructive example of the thinking of a student who had reached Piaget's third stage but not the fourth, yet who clearly was struggling earnestly to do arithmetic, is this paper written by a girl who was asked by her teacher to write down how she decided whether to add, subtract, multiply, or divide. She wrote: "If there are lots of numbers I add. If there are only 2 numbers with lots of parts I subtract. But if there are just 2 numbers and one a little harder than the other then it is a hard problem so I divide if they come out even, but if they don't I multiply."

Developmental sequence: moral reasoning

Another developmental sequence on the journey from childhood to adulthood is levels and stages of moral reasoning — the ability to think about right and wrong, truth and falsehood, good and bad.

Lawrence Kohlberg, a psychologist at Harvard, has observed and identified the stages through which people go in a fixed sequence; it is not possible to skip a stage.[1] Kohlberg has also found that people in quite different cultures go through the same fixed sequence. But different people proceed at different rates, and most people stop at a certain stage and go no farther. Home and school have direct influence on the rate of progress through the stages as well as on how far a person's ability for moral reasoning will develop.

As you read the explanation that follows, it may help you to look at the chart of levels, stages, and typical ages shown below.

---

[1]This account is adapted from my book *How To Live through Junior High School*, new ed. (Philadelphia: Lippincott, 1975), pp. 34-38, which, in turn, is based on Lawrence Kohlberg and Carol Gilligan, "The Adolescent as Philosopher: The Discovery of the Self in a Postconventional World," *Daedalus*, fall 1971, pp. 1051-1086.

Kohlberg's Stages of Moral Reasoning

Stage 0. The good is what I like	0-4 years

Preconventional level

Stage 1. Avoid punishment	4-7
Stage 2. You be nice; I'll be nice	7-10

Conventional level

Stage 3. Good boy, good girl	9-11
Stage 4. Law and order; rules and obedience	11-15 and up

Postconventional level

Stage 5a. Voluntary agreements, determined for self and faithfully held	Adolescence (about 14) and up
Stage 5b. Individual sense of right and wrong; conscience as a higher law	After adolescence
Stage 6. Sacredness of life as a universal value	Rarely shown; fullest moral maturity

During the first four years or so, the child displays no "moral" reasoning, but simply knows or feels that "what I want and like is good." Then, at about age four, as the child enters nursery school, he or she reaches the first of three major levels, the *preconventional level*. This is the level, or time, before the rules of group living or of society become a direct force upon the child's life. Of the two stages at this level, stage 1 consists simply of avoiding punishment: if I am frowned at, scolded, or hit, I don't do it; if I am smiled at, praised, or patted, I do it. The stage 1 child defers to superior power. Stage 2 of moral reasoning is based on the fairness of sharing: I'll be nice to you because then you'll be nice to me; you scratch my back, I'll scratch yours.

The preconventional level lasts, among most middle-class American children, through grade 4 or 5. Some people never go beyond stage 2, however, and many regress to it in times of stress, as in adolescence. Some, on the other hand, go beyond it earlier than grade 4 or 5.

The second major level of moral reasoning is the *conven-*

tional level, during which people reason according to what they think society expects of them. Stage 3 is "the way I'm supposed to be" stage, when the child wants to be a good girl or a good boy. "Moral" is what receives approval and gets you liked. Stage 4 is the law and order stage, where people believe in fixed rules and respect authority. Theirs is the reasoning of the Ten Commandments, not the Golden Rule. Most Americans probably never go beyond this stage, even some very intelligent and successful ones who would argue that there is no better way to arrange society.

Those who enter the third major level of moral reasoning, the *postconventional level,* do so through questioning the accepted rules and conventions and working out for themselves moral principals based on their own convictions, not on what someone else has told them is right. Kohlberg has found it necessary to divide stage 5 into two parts. Stage 5a consists of agreements and obligations freely entered into and faithfully held. The writers of the United States Constitution seem to have operated by this stage of moral reasoning. (Obviously, good teaching and reading and discussion would help a person move from stage 4 to stage 5.) Stage 5b is a morality based on individual conscience, an inner sense of right and wrong, even though the actions it dictates may go against what is considered community welfare or the rules of society. Kohlberg says that stage 6 morality, seen only in rare individuals, is based on "belief in the sacredness of human life as representing a universal human value" and deep commitment to that belief. Such figures as Buddha, Jesus, Hillel, Gandhi, and Martin Luther King come to mind as representing this highest stage of morality. Doubtless there are many others, too, most of them living out their lives without ever becoming famous.

Relating Kohlberg to Piaget

Kohlberg's stages of moral reasoning relate to Piaget's stages of logical thinking. As you might expect, it is impossible for people to pass beyond stage 4, the law and order stage of morality, until they have moved into Piaget's period of formal operations, when abstract thinking and a high order of questioning are possible. This passage is likely to come with the passage through adolescence. The "adolescent" thinker is one who, finding old barriers tottering, has to rebuild, to think anew, to find himself again, to establish new relationships with all aspects of his world, including the physical and mental world inside himself.

This process makes waves, a rough passage — much rougher for some than for others. The breakdown of the desire to look like a good boy or girl and of the established order of rules and respect causes stress. We all know that under stress we often regress to more childish behavior. So early adolescents, under the stress of the rough passage, may seem to regress to earlier stages of moral reasoning, a sort of relapse into what appears to be stage 2 — mutual backscratching — but only for a while, a sort of backsliding needed for a move forward to new levels of maturity. Some people think that Kohlberg should have included stage 4½, the stage of adolescent relapse and relativistic crisis.

Remember, Kohlberg's stages are steps in the development of moral reasoning, not necessarily moral behavior. The ability to reason in the Kohlberg sense is a necessary condition to moral behavior, but our actions do not always come up to the best we know, no matter how old we are.

Clearly, we must keep these developmental stages of thinking and moral reasoning in mind — or at least the concept of growth in stages — if we are to fit our instruction to the various conditions of our students. It is especially important to understand that discussion, rather than up-front, teacher-dominated instruction, best helps students to move through these stages.

Instruction and reading

Before going on to talk about discussion, I should say a word about the most vital skill: reading. I don't know enough to explain how to teach reading to beginners; that is a special skill. But once children have learned how to translate printed and written letters into speech and then into ideas, they do need instruction, accompanied by discussion and practice, in the often unrecognized fact that there are several kinds of reading.

Too many students, and probably most adults, believe that there is only one way to read, one that is far too slow and plodding for most material and yet not slow and careful enough for some other kinds of material. All teachers should therefore be alert for opportunities to instruct and to demonstrate that there are at least five types of reading, and that the nature of the assignment and the material should determine the type to be used. Here are the five types.

1. *Skimming*, for a general overview of the material or to find specific items of information.

2. *Rapid, relaxed reading*, to enjoy a story or account of something you are interested in.

3. *Close, active reading*, for mastery, used with textbooks, encyclopedias, and other materials from which you must learn main facts and ideas.

4. *Word-for-word reading*, perhaps aloud, for directions or for math and science problems.

5. *Poetry reading*, best done aloud, for meaning, metaphor, feeling, sound.

In giving your students an assignment, take time to discuss with them what type of reading they think they should use and to show them, if need be, how the types of reading differ.

One special sort of reading that can be used to good and bad effect in the classroom is reading aloud. Perhaps you feel that students will be helped if they get a feel for the rhythm and sound of a particular writer's work. If so, prepare yourself to read very well a passage or two aloud. To do this is usually much better than simply assigning the passage to read at home without clues to its difficulties and delights.

Never require students to read aloud to the entire class unless you know they are good oral readers. Even though you can often tell quite a lot about the state of students' reading by hearing them read aloud, some students find oral reading a difficult and embarrassing task. This is especially true if the rest of the class laughs at errors, which they may well do, because some errors are really funny — but not to the reader who is making them. Furthermore, being able to read aloud is no proof of a person's ability to read silently.

So if you do want something to be read aloud and feel that a voice other than yours should do the reading (for teachers' voices are heard too much), call on somebody who likes to read aloud and is good at it.

Giving directions

As a rule, teachers give directions too fast and unclearly for the students who don't understand and too slowly for those who get bored and turned off. You can save everyone a lot of grief and work if you think out carefully in advance how you are going to give directions. Here are some pointers.

• Make your directions clear and present them in steps. As you go from point to point, write each one on the board, in full or in abbreviated form. Leave the written directions on the board so that slower people can refer to them later.

• After each point, or at the end, ask "Is that clear?" If it isn't, explain again in a different way. Don't repeat unless it is necessary. So many of us repeat so much that students learn not to look or listen the first time.

• When you're pretty sure that most people know what to do, say that you'll explain further at the end of the period, for those who need it, and leave time to do so.

• If the assignment extends beyond one day, you can ask again, the second day, whether anyone is having problems with it. Don't go over it all again; just explain the parts that aren't clear.

• Work out as many routines as possible so that after the first few days you don't need to give directions on such matters as the form of papers, where to hand them in, what to do about a late paper, and when and where to get individual help.

6.
Learning the Basics: Discussion and Mastery

Hint 3. To teach is not to simplify every step until there is no real work for the child to do.
Abbie G. Hall

The best way to use classroom time is in discussion, which is about the only thing that can't be done just as well or better somewhere else.

First, let's be clear about two things that discussion is not. It is not reciting memorized facts, and it is not the class trying to guess an answer that is hidden in the teacher's mind — a rather low form of activity and dull to boot.

Conditions essential for genuine discussion

Good discussion occurs when questions that do not have a yes or no answer are put to the class and the teacher steps back to let thinking and exchange of ideas and opinions take place. Because the number of good questions for discussion is infinite, you should have little trouble formulating some that grow naturally out of the subject your class is studying.

If we are going to have good class discussions, we must overcome our fear of silence, especially since some of the most educational time spent in the classroom is spent in the silence of thinking as part of discussion. Too many of us, when we encounter a question to which there is no ready answer, shortcut the educational process by calling on the first hand raised by or accepting the first blurt.

When a good question is before an attentive class ("Is violence ever the best way to settle a problem?" "How can fiction be truer than nonfiction?" "Will pocket calculators help you be

a better mathematician?''), then come the moments of intense education — unless the intensity is sprung by a blurt or, worse, by the teacher giving *an* answer that is taken as *the* answer.

It is far better to put the question and wait — ten, even fifteen, seconds, a long time in most classrooms, but a thin slice of the thick hours of a school day — until several hands are up, with everybody thinking, and then to call on one person to speak. Those post-question silences are the best and the rarest in schools.

To have this kind of discussion, you need to make sure the class understands that no one is to speak without raising a hand and being recognized. Letting people speak as soon as they have a thought interrupts the others and allows fast thinkers and confident talkers to dominate the discussion. Those who think more carefully or thoroughly may have some good ideas, too. It is very important that spirited conversation among the teacher and the four or five quickest students not be confused with genuine class discussion.

An important skill for presiding over a discussion is being able to turn a question back to the class instead of giving the answer, which we are so used to doing and so expected by our classes to do. For example, if in discussing hand raising a student says, "But I don't see why we can't speak when we have an idea. If we can't, it makes it so stiff, like," you can, instead of explaining why, say "Well, why not?" and, after that, "Is it going to make things stiff and uncomfortable?" and let the answers arise from the class.

Techniques and arrangements

Here are several suggestions for conducting a class discussion.

- Don't repeat a student's comment. It is all too common for teachers to repeat or paraphrase, in a loud, clear voice, what a student has said so that everyone will be sure to hear and understand it clearly. But this is a harmful practice, for it says to students that they don't need to speak up, but only to the teacher, who will be the source of all truth.
- Don't dominate the discussion. Your main function in a discussion is to preside over an exchange of ideas and opinions, and to keep students talking with students. Whatever ques-

tions you ask should be for the purpose of keeping the group on the subject and thinking with greater clarity. The art is in asking questions, or getting students to ask questions, that require clarification of ideas and move the class toward resolving the issue being discussed. One exception to your not making comments arises when a timid student who needs encouragement finally does say something quite good and everybody passes it by out of habit. Here's a chance to build the student up a bit, not just by saying, "Good, Jamie," but by taking his idea and showing its worth by adding an example or stating another dimension of it, perhaps ending with a question, like, "What else can you think of that shows that Jamie has made a really key point?"

• Don't always call on the first student whose hand goes up. Allow time for several hands to go up. Perhaps you'll call on the last one up, that of the less bold contributor who needs encouragement, or the one who arrives at the talking point more slowly than the others.

• Move desks into a circle or a U. After all, it is much harder to have an all-class discussion if you can't see anybody's face but the teacher's without turning around. It's worth taking the time to move the furniture.

• When a student is talking, move away from him, not closer. This will make his voice carry across more of the entire group, if you are moving about the class during the discussion. (I happen to think it's usually better to stay seated with the others.) And avoid private exchanges with and between individual students, which tend to be inaudible to the rest of the class.

• Always ask a question before naming a person to answer it. "What are some advantages of having opposable thumbs . . . [ten-second wait], John?" not "John, what are . . . ?" The first way makes everyone think about the question, not just John.

• Never call on students in any predictable order, for that will guarantee a low percentage of involvement.

• Keep track of who has spoken and who has not. If some students have not taken part at all during the period, or for several periods, look for ways to involve them, perhaps by calling on them even if they don't raise their hands but you think they may have something to say. You might even think up an "easy" question to ask and then call on the quiet person or ask him to report on a familiar and relevant experience.

• But never invade students' privacy. All students have a right to be silent, and we teachers have no right to insist that they relate their experiences. We do, however, have a right, perhaps a duty, to put some pressure on them to answer questions on material they have been assigned to answer. That can be good motivation for future effort, but it's not really discussion; it's recitation.

• Allow an occasional outburst of comment or reaction. If some nonrecognized student makes a statement that stimulates almost everyone to talk and you find that the class has become a noisy jumble of excited comments, let it happen for a few moments. Often really good communication and exchange go on at such times. After the buzz has died down, say something like, "Well, Mary, that really got a reaction. Let's discuss it. Any hands?"

• Small-group discussions are often better than all-class ones. If there are twenty-five to thirty-five students or more in your class, it is hard to maintain interest and general participation in a discussion. Breaking the class into small groups of five or six each works well and gives everyone a much better chance to participate. Each small group needs a discussion leader; you have to be able to move the chairs so that the groups can cluster around the room; and it is a good idea to write the discussion question on the board so that each group can refer to it. It also helps to give the groups "tasks" to accomplish: (1) Be ready to report on one or two ideas that the group has agreed on; (2) Be ready to state several interesting facts or experiences that relate to the subject; or (3) Try to state and report on the two or three most interesting opinions that came up. The group leaders should be ready to speak for their groups right after the end of the discussion. Note that a summary of the discussion — which is almost always dull and trite — is not called for.

Some benefits of discussion

From good discussions come important benefits that constitute learning or developing many of the basics listed in Chapter

4. People develop the skill and habit of listening. They learn to express themselves and to stand up for their ideas better and with greater confidence. The class learns to do a better job of exchanging ideas and communicating. People learn to let their minds be opened and changed as they hear and take in new ideas.

Further, discussion trains students to question and seek answers — to think — and not to accept unthinkingly as truth statements and assertions made by others, a skill especially necessary for citizens in a democracy. Discussion can reveal aspects, dimensions, and possibilities of an assignment that are less likely to emerge if merely explained by the teacher.

Finally, discussion shows you, the teacher, and the class how people are thinking and feeling, what sort of people they are, what turns them on, and what sorts of ideas and experience they have.

Mastery of fundamentals

Some schools pass students from grade to grade without ever giving them the opportunity, much less requiring them, to master the skills they need in order to go on successfully. Consequently, many students fall farther and farther behind and get more and more turned off by school until, at last, they drop out, or, if resources and motivation are present, they are given strenuous, expensive remedial work to catch them up.

It seems to me that those students who are not mastering the fundamentals are the ones who should have the first-priority attention of teachers. In the long run, this will save everyone time and trouble and make more time for "creative" work as the gap closes between those who have mastered and those who have not. The following four steps in teaching for mastery are not original, but they can be helpful.

1. *Presentation of material.* The presentation should consist of a variety of methods and materials, not just teacher talk and assignments in books. After all, not everyone learns best by listening and reading.

2. *Participation and evaluation.* Students need many opportunities to practice what they are learning. As they learn, most students — especially young ones and timid ones — need

something that tells them how they're doing: a word of praise, a good score, a job obviously completed and mastered, even a gold star or a line going up on a progress chart, or the chance to explain to others, to help and be helped as the effort to learn is shared. At this stage, marks — many marks — can be helpful. I believe that marks, or grades, properly used, give accurate information, a quick measure of success or lack of it, a sense of accomplishment, and understanding of where you stand in relation to mastering the subject and what you need to do next. (See Chapter 21 for fuller discussion of marks.) The poorest and least confident, least competent students need the most participation and evaluation. In most schools, they get the least.

3. *Testing.* Here we are speaking of a real test, not the kind of testing involved in the previous step. The test may be a well-devised assignment or a set of questions that each student tackles alone, under supervision, that show whether or not he or she has mastered the fundamentals. (See Chapters 15-17.)

4. *Further teaching.* Too many teachers stop with the third step, above. They record a grade and hand back the test, which shows whether or not the student has mastered the material. That being that, the class moves on to the next phase of the subject. But that should not be that! Instead, primary attention should be given to those who have failed to master the essentials. This should involve several activities: reteaching, allowing those who know the material to help those who don't, working out fresh ways to explain, assigning new reading and exercises, giving special help in small groups and to individuals, and testing again when you think most of those who failed now know the material.

It's important not to punish those who haven't mastered the material, unless you are sure they did so simply out of pure laziness — but laziness is seldom pure, or simple. It is important, also, not just to repeat the same teaching process that failed to result in learning the first time.

One example of how to deal with failure I found in a most unlikely place, Temple Medical School, in Philadelphia, where one of my children is studying. Because one essential for practicing medicine is a thorough knowledge of anatomy, much of the first year is taken up with its study. After each major anatomy test, the 10 to 15 per cent of the class who fail the test are given a special privilege: the hottest-shot professor of anatomy holds special sessions for this group, dissecting a cadaver and brilliantly explaining as he goes along everything that they may not have understood when they were dissecting their cadavers. The class is closed; only those who failed the test, a small enough group to make real question-and-answer teaching possible, are allowed to attend. Afterwards, most of them pass the test. They have learned the fundamentals, and they are ready to proceed.

What does the teacher do with those who have mastered the material when so much special attention is needed by those who haven't? The answers, briefly, are enrichment, individual projects for the able, grouping students so that some parts of the work are still done by everyone together and other parts assigned to individuals or groups, and making homework assignments that are broad enough so that the amount of time it takes depends on the interest, ability, and individual time the student has.

This all sounds much simpler than it really is. The simplest thing, of course, is to give everybody the same work and to teach everybody the same thing in class. The better way can be managed, however, and by ordinary people who aren't geniuses or slaves to their jobs.

7.
Planning a Year and a Unit

Hint 24. Pupils grow and develop by what they do themselves, not by what their teacher does for them.   *Abbie G. Hall*

In a moment of enthusiasm, a committee earnestly stated in its minutes, "This year we are going to concentrate on everything." That sentence tells exactly why teaching can be the hardest, the most rewarding, and the most inherently frustrating job there is: because teachers have to try to concentrate on everything and be aware of everything all at once, even though such concentration is impossible.

One part of our concentration must be on the state of mind, body, spirit, and experience of each of our pupils' experience past, present, and in a near or distant future. Another part is our colleagues in the complex institution where we work. Still another is the community of which our school is a part — both parents and public. And then, of course, we must concentrate on the subject matter we teach. That is the topic of this chapter.

Planning a year's work

I've usually taught in schools where I had too much freedom to decide what I would teach. As a beginner, I underestimated the importance of having a coherent scheme for the year, feeling that the subject and I should evolve as the students evolved.

I have learned that it works better for the students and for me when I plan in advance the year's scheme of content, materials, and activities from which, when the way opens, we may depart. The subject matter is not the most important element;

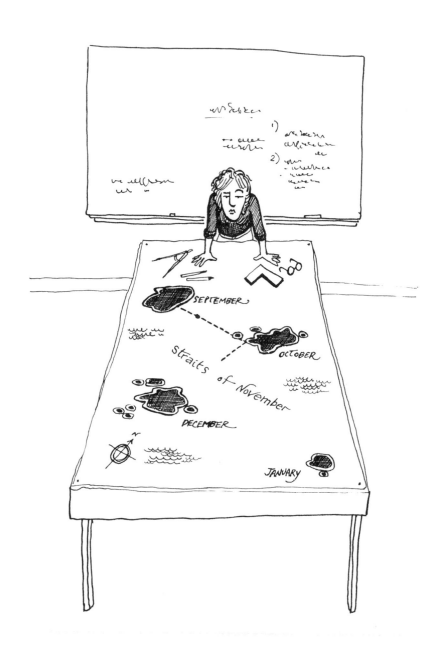

developing each student into a happy and useful person is. However, I believe that this all-important development takes place best, in schools, as a by-product of dealing with the subject matter. We teach subjects, and the whole business affects students.

In most schools, teachers are given a curriculum to teach that is supplied with objectives, divided into units, and furnished with materials. Teachers should become thoroughly familiar with all the elements of this curriculum before the year begins and make their own plans and arrangements for teaching it. They should try to foresee where their own knowledge can usefully supplement texts and other materials and, where their knowledge is inadequate, they need to prepare themselves by filling in the gaps. No teacher should worry about not knowing everything, however. Learning *with* students is good for everyone, provided it's not overdone. Students respect both a teacher's knowledge and his or her willingness to admit gaps in it.

One of the main problems of a year's work, especially for teachers in the upper grades, is the compulsion to "cover" a certain amount of material. This compulsion, combined with an equal compulsion to be thorough, sometimes leads us into the situation of the Vassar student in the cartoon who, frantically writing an exam, glances at the clock and cries, "My God, only five minutes left and three centuries to go!"

We should realize that, while no subject ever gets entirely "covered," it is important for students to feel the satisfaction of having learned a complete section of it. The surveys of American history that never get beyond World War I arc not satisfactory. More important than coverage, in any case, is to develop the feeling in students that they want to know more and that they have to *do* the subject, not just memorize it.

A vital part of planning for the year involves thinking carefully about how you are going to help students develop basic skills and attitudes as you work with them and the subject matter. If the school's written curriculum does not list these basics and integrate them into the subjects taught, you would do well to make your own informal list. One example is the collection of basics set forth in Chapter 5.

Even experienced teachers should take a fresh, honest look

each year at what they are teaching to see how adequate and realistic their objectives are and how well they think they are being achieved. Teachers need to devise measures other than intuition and wishful thinking — and suitable to their discipline and style — to reveal what there students are achieving. Some suggestions are given in Chapters 15-17 and 19.

Planning a unit of work

As work on skills and attitudes continues throughout the year, students at most grade levels will benefit by the sense of progress they gain by proceeding from unit to unit of subject matter, even if it is only from one chapter or unit in a textbook to the next. Most students like to feel they are starting something new now and then, not just keeping on with the same old thing.

Here, simply as an example, is the group of units I have worked out for a year of eighth-grade English.

Unit 1. *Mechanics and procedures.* A brief explanation and discussion of how the year's work will go, a quick look at the materials to be used, discussion of the skills and attitudes to be developed, all combined with an initial writing assignment in which students say something about who they are and what they hope or think they will need to get out of the course. I explain that this paper will provide a sample of their writing to give me an idea of what people in the class know about writing and what they need to learn and that it will give me some idea of them and their ideas. After I read the papers (and read parts of them to the class), we all discuss procedures for dealing with written work.

Unit 2. *The short story.* Reading several stories from an anthology and writing one.

Unit 3. *To Kill a Mockingbird,* by Harper Lee. Reading and discussing the book, with a test at the end, part on facts, part writing answers to questions.

Unit 4. *The English language.* Brief history of the language and how it has evolved in the context of other languages and study of how languages get their words, with a chance to coin some words, using authentic methods.

Unit 5. *The War of the Worlds,* by H. G. Wells. Similar to unit 3.

Unit 6. *Poetry.* Reading from a short, varied anthology, discussing and demonstrating what makes a poem, and writing any kind of poetry (including limericks and parodies) the students want to write. The unit ends with a test of recognition and understanding of poetry, reading some of the best student poems, and each student handing in a collection of his or her poems.

Unit 7. *Sex education.* A month of information giving and reading (with a test of facts), discussion of all the issues that interest the students, and writing a paper on a topic related to human sexuality. (I must point out that sex education is not usually or necessarily a part of eighth-grade English, except at our school, but it's as much "English" as it is anything else.)

Unit 8. *Great Expectations,* by Charles Dickens. Similar to unit 3.

Unit 9. *Pantomime-speechmaking and autobiography.* A combination of two rather unrelated subjects, one of which takes a lot of class time, the other a lot of homework time. The unit starts with a carefully made long assignment of an autobiography. While students are working on that at home, in class they prepare and perform either pantomimes (in the Marcel Marceau mode) or a prepared speech on any subject, spoken from notes but not read. The speech and pantomime part of the unit may end up as a public performance before some group in school.

While this collection of units may seem like an almost totally unrelated congeries, all parts of it do have to do with the skills of English and the problems and delights of being human. It really doesn't matter much whether or not you have a great theme that arches over all the units in a year's work. Very often, the generalization represented by such a theme exists only in the mind of the teacher. The important thing is to make the units interesting and to provide ample materials and activities for learning.

I have found that it often makes little difference in what order units are taught, except the first one, and possibly the last. Usually, if I have three or four sections of the same grade, I teach a different unit to each section during given weeks or months so that my life will be more varied. That way, I have different papers to read at different times and in smaller batches, and I feel no pressure to keep all four sections going along at exactly the same rate.

Some teachers, however, prefer to unify the work of the entire year under a single theme: the Pilgrims, ecology, ancient Egypt, the family. Teachers in lower and middle grades sometimes use a non-subject-matter motif to give coherence and interest to the year's work: an African village (with tribes and subtribes), a voyage by ship, a zoo. Care is needed to make sure that the motif is not carried to extremes or into realms of stereotype or ignorance.

Now, let's return to the problem of planning the year's units regardless of theme or motif. In general, a unit should begin with an activity to stimulate the students' interest. It should then provide materials and work that will maintain that interest and teach the subject matter. A unit should be so constructed that it will provide some success to the least able and some challenge to the most gifted. It should be completed with some sort of culminating event, whether a performance, a discussion, a film accompanied by a writing assignment, or just a challenging final test.

Short elective courses

Another type of unit into which the school year can be broken is the four- to eight-week elective course. Often such courses are open, say, to students in grades 6-8, or in grades 10-12, so that they can be taught by a relatively small core group of teachers who concentrate on a relatively small group of students and get to know them quite well as the year proceeds.

Under this arrangement, teachers teach the same students, in different combinations, in more than one elective course. This is important, because otherwise the teacher who works with students for only a few weeks and then doesn't see them again can't become familiar enough with their strengths and weaknesses to help them develop their skills and attitudes.

The following examples of the sorts of mini-electives that a school might offer to students in grades 6-8 are taken from the curriculums of schools I have visited.

Generation Link:	Solar Energy
Genetics	Topology
The Incredible Machine:	Introduction to
Human Anatomy	Analytic Geometry

Making a Literary
  Magazine
Basic English Grammar
Fellowship of the Ring, by
  J. R. R. Tolkien
Sherlock Holmes
Science Fiction
Writing from Pictures
Writing a Term Paper
How Mankind Adapts:
  Anthropology
Human Sexuality:
  Information and
  Issues
Old China and *The Good
  Earth*, by Pearl S. Buck
Making the Constitution
Geography of the Western
  United States
Historiography and
  Computers
The School Campus as an
  Archaeological Site

Concord, Massachusetts,
  and the Revolution
Problems in Our
  Neighborhood:
  Developing an Action
  Program
Machines and Libraries
Library Organization and
  Services
Physical Conditioning
Gymnastics
Creative Exercise and
  Movement
Sight Singing
Opera
Music History I, II, III, etc.
Printmaking
Drawing
Sculpture
Puppets and Plays
Elementary Carpentry
What Makes an Engine
  Run?

Any ambitious, flexible group of teachers examining their own interests, knowledge, and expertise can develop a group of electives like the ones above to appeal to students of whatever age.

What I said earlier about planning a unit as part of a year-long course also goes for short electives. The advantages of electives are several. Because students take electives by choice, they tend to be more interested and work harder than in regular courses. This attitude makes it easier to go quite deeply into an especially well-defined area of subject matter. Groupings in electives change every four to eight weeks, so it is easier to section students by ability without the usual negative overtones, and to tailor each student's program to meet his or her particular needs and interests. And students can, to some extent, choose not only what courses they will take but also which teachers they will have.

While most teachers who have tried small elective courses are enthusiastic, a number of disadvantages do need to be considered. Teachers who teach a group for only eight weeks and not again never get to know their students well. By the time they know who needs what, the unit is over and they don't have time to take advantage of this knowledge. Thus, the courses may be too strongly subject-oriented and not enough student-oriented, making it difficult to follow up on students' needs and weaknesses.

Foreign languages, math, science, and group music — subjects that require sustained, cumulative development of skills and knowledge — are less appropriate for inclusion in a mini-elective system. Short courses require considerably more time, effort, and ingenuity on the part of teachers than conventional year-long ones, first, because teachers are likely to spend more time preparing an elective for a new group of students, and, second, because having to reschedule students every eight weeks and all that that involves is challenging, time-consuming, and complicated.

Here are a few suggestions, based on experience, that can help you make the most of a mini-elective system and minimize its disadvantages.

• Most of the courses offered should be taught by a fairly small core of teachers who come to know the students well because they teach them several times during the year. There is a place for teachers from outside the core who have an attractive, interesting special single course to teach to a single group — and this can be very refreshing — but if more than a third of the teaching is done by non-core teachers, this piecemeal approach can be harmful to the steady development of students over the course of the year. (This is less likely to happen, of course, with highly motivated, self-directed students who have skills well in hand and enjoy change.)

• The core faculty should meet at least once a week to discuss the program and share information about the needs of their students so that when the time comes they can pass along to the new group of teachers whatever they know in order to ensure continuity of individual student development.

• In a large school, in the grades to which electives are given, students should be organized in units ("houses," "colleges," "companies," "associations") that are small enough for all of the core faculty to know each member of the group to play an active part in monitoring and guiding each student's progress. Five core teachers for a "house" of 150 students is about the smallest number that can give really sustained, enlightened attention to a group that size; ten teachers would be better.

• Each student's records should be easily available to all teachers at the beginning of the course so that the teachers may pick up important facts they need in order to teach their students as well as possible. The core group should devise a system for easy, up-to-date collection of and access to relevant grades, scores, and anecdotal material — the kind of information that teachers who teach a class all year long normally have in their gradebooks and their heads.

• If students are to benefit from the full range of courses available to them, they need ample guidance in choosing courses and teachers. The core teachers should be familiar with all the courses available and especially familiar with the situations, interests, and abilities of the students who are assigned to them for guidance. Some students do best taking lots of courses with the same teacher, while others need variety; some should be steered away from (or toward) courses involving a great deal of reading and independent work; and some would benefit from trying a new area but need encouragement to do so.

• The core faculty, with one person acting as editor, should make available accurate, brief, consistent descriptions of each elective in printed form. Each description should include the course title, the teacher's name, a short listing of course content and activities and information about reading, homework, and required papers, and mention of any other courses that might be useful prerequisites or sequels.

• Care should be taken to see that each student chooses a good distribution of courses during the year so that no one will, for example, escape all science or take nothing but science. The faculty should work out a set of minimum distribution requirements and required courses that it is willing to discuss with students and ready to change as circumstances change.

8.
Planning a Class Period

Hint 2. If you would keep a bright pupil out of mischief give him enough to do.
Abbie G. Hall

This chapter concerns planning for the single period, which in most schools lasts 45-50 minutes and within which most teachers in the middle and upper grades do their teaching.

There are so many different kinds of schools and classes that the suggestions I am about to make may not fit any of them. Many of the ideas that I have developed or been taught by others have helped me, however, so some of them may help you.

A typical workable lesson plan

First and most important, for each class period, is a plan, either scribbled down in your own brand of shorthand or carefully written out, to get you and the class through from beginning to end. Following are items from a seventh-grade English class plan, which, while not a perfect plan, does illustrate some key points.

A. Write something on the board for the class to start working on. Always put this in the same place so that students will develop the habit of looking there.

B. Note various reminders to yourself of people and things that need attention whenever convenient during the period.

C. Start the period by letting people who have problems bring them up for discussion. If a problem is of general interest, discuss it with the whole class. If it only concerns the person who raised it, deal with it briefly and offer to see the person at the end of the period (and remember to do this). Keep this question period moving unless problems are general and serious, in which case you may need to abandon part of the lesson plan in order to get the class on track and motivated.

D. Remind the class of any imminent deadlines — poetry assignment, handing in individual reading notebooks, and so on.

E. Reinforce any spelling rules (and two demons) that have shown up through errors made by several people in the past day or two.

F. Following up on an earlier promise, ask whether anyone wants to read his or her own poems to the class. (Usually, no one does.)

G. Now the really new stuff of the lesson begins. Some days, it is better to start off at this point, omitting the earlier items or working them in later. It all depends on the mood of the class, what students expect, how interested they are in the material, and what you've been doing the two or three days before. Some classes like a change of pace; others do better with an unvarying pattern that makes them feel reassured.

H. Note the questions you want to ask the class. Asking good, varied general and specific questions is one of the most important skills of teaching.

I. Following H, ask the class how, for example, poetry should be read aloud, illustrating it with one poem and reinforcing it with another.

J. For a change of pace, plan a short written assignment to be done in class and save time to read some examples aloud.

K. In case the period hasn't ended (usually it has by this time), have enough games or activities ready that will take as little or as much time as you need.

The six most important points covered by this lesson plan are that (1) it is definite and purposeful, (2) it allows students to bring up problems that may be causing difficulty in their long-term work, (3) it contains more material than you can possibly cover yet does not seem cut off if not completed, (4) it covers new specific material while referring to previous ideas and skills and looking forward to new ones, (5) it gives every member of the class, whether nimble or slow, an opportunity to participate, and (6) it offers enough change of pace so that the class is unlikely to get bored.

Arranging and teaching a class period

Developing study skills and arranging for homework, or independent work, are obviously vital ingredients of the class period and of the year's work in school. Before discussing them in the next two chapters, however, I want to suggest a few more ideas for helping you plan your work.

• Establish routines. The sooner you set up basic routines for getting materials, handing in work, arranging conferences, breaking into small groups, and finding homework assignments, the more freedom you and the class will have for teaching and learning. Always be open to students' ideas for better ways to carry out routines.

• Every period may be a fresh start for someone in the class. To maintain a truly professional and humane attitude toward each pupil, each teacher must simultaneously teach with all the school's past experience with that pupil in mind and allow constantly for the possibility that a student may, under our influence, or the influence of the summer, or of internal juices, be reborn — any day, any minute. If you are going to err in your plans for a student, err on the side of optimism and high expectations.

• Don't worry about unfinished discussion. Learning and thought do not stop when the bell rings. If what has happened during class has stimulated interest, that may have been its main value, even if you never get back to the question again. If the bell does ring when you are all in the middle of talking about academic work or bad human relations in the class, however, make a note to yourself to give it first priority the next day.

• Save lesson plans that work well. Some teachers, at the end of the year, virtuously throw away all their old lesson plans, tests, and devices with the admirable purpose of avoiding staleness, doing it better next year, being open to new ways. Heaven forbid that they ever do anything the same way twice. My advice: if a book, test, plan, game, exercise works well, keep it and use it again. For several years, I taught the same three books to the eighth grade. They all worked well; I developed and refined good multiple-choice tests on each; I found which discussion questions were provocative; I invented written assignments that stimulated good writing. I became so familiar with the material that I was liberated — liberated to observe my students, attend to their needs, see them after school. Once knowing the subject matter, I was freed to know my students.

• Don't be afraid to toss out your plan and ask, "All right, what would you like to talk about today?" If you let your students know that you will be doing this occasionally, some of them may come to you in advance and say, "Can't we talk about . . . sometime?" and you can make whatever it is part of your plan within the next few days.

• Plan to finish class business early from time to time so that you can declare a relaxed moment for the class to talk freely, with you circulating about the room.

• Have a sign-up place on the blackboard for people who want or need to confer with you about a problem or individual business, like a puzzling math problem. Or you can write someone's name there if you need to see him. This way, nobody has to wait in line; when one name is crossed off the list, the next person comes to confer.

• Everyone should always have independent work to do — some reading, or writing, or whatever — if a few free minutes crop up. For those who forget to come prepared, have a collection of books and activities.

• Develop some foolproof time passers in case plans fail, half the class gets held in gym, or textbooks don't come, or just if life looks too grim for regular work.

• Identify as many students' problems as early as you can, so that you and your colleagues can get to work on them. Altogether too many teachers say, each year, "Oh, I never look at a student's record. I want to give each one a fresh start and not be biased." Which means that they don't find out until it is too late who is a poor reader and who a good one; who always slumps between Christmas and midyear unless held firm; who is dumb and acts bright, who is bright and acts dumb, who does neither (as far as we can tell from scores and anecdotal records); who works best when left alone; who would be turned on if you'd just come out to cheer at the game after school; who needs to talk but is too shy to say so. Ignoring such matters means that too much essential information is rediscovered only by January, fully understood in February, and brought to the point of action in March, by which time it is so close to June that we decide just to write a note about it for next year's teachers. We have no right to repeat such mistakes. It is unprofessional, inefficient, and not even respectful. It is much better to discover problems that need remedial action in October so that we will have time to diagnose the trouble, prescribe treatment, and get to work.

9.
Study Skills

> *Hint 93.* In the lower grades never tell pupils
> to study until you have told them what to do
> and how to do it.   *Abbie G. Hall*

When students are assigned independent work, without the teacher or anyone else to supervise, they should be thrown on their own to do the work in their own way and according to their own plans. They often need help with this, however. Many students need to be taught some study skills, which is another term for "how to learn." Others, who seem to know how to study from the very start, are naturally bored to death by study-habit formulas.

A statement for students

Here is a statement on study skills that works for students between grades 4 and 12.[1] You can teach it piecemeal, which might be best for fourth graders, or hand it out to each student and then discuss it with anyone who shows signs that he or she might benefit from it. It should not be forced on anyone.

Study Skills

How to "study" is not a simple lesson, easily learned. Also, each person has his or her own style of learning. Some work in bursts, some plod along systematically. Some reason along straight lines of logic, some leap intuitively from insight to insight.

---

[1] This statement is adapted from my book *How To Live through Junior High School*, new ed. (Philadelphia: Lippincott, 1975), pp. 96-101. Any teacher wishing to duplicate the statement for students' use is specifically granted permission to do so herewith. E. W. J.

If you are not doing well in school, or are doing well but could be doing even better, this list of study techniques may help you. You probably won't want to use them all, but some will almost certainly be useful to you.

1. *Write down assignments,* with date due, clearly, promptly, in a regular place, preferably a small homework notebook, not on just any available scrap of paper. If you aren't sure what the assignment means, ask the teacher.

2. *Have a regular schedule for home study.* You can probably work better after dinner than before. When you return from school, your mind needs a rest and your body some food and exercise. However, styles and rhythms of brainwork and body work differ.

3. *Have a regular place for study* equipped with pencils, pen, paper, scissors, ruler, dictionary, calendar, and a good lamp. Occasionally, though, an escape from the regular place can provide new inspiration — under a tree? on the roof?

4. *Be certain of the purpose of an assignment before you do it.* Ask yourself, "What am I supposed to learn from this? Why was it assigned to me?" Teachers almost always have a particular goal in mind when they give an assignment. What is it? If you don't know, ask tactfully.

5. *Skim over any reading assignment rapidly before reading it closely.* Glance at the main headings and titles, or paragraph beginnings, to get a general idea of what it's about and to help you relate the ideas to the main topic and to the rest of the course, and to whatever other knowledge you have, when you read the chapter closely later. This skimming shouldn't take more than four or five minutes for a 15- to 20-page chapter.

6. *Use any study aids in the book* if you have some close reading to do. Note the chapter title, which will probably give you the main idea, and the headings of the main sections. If there are italicized words, read them with special care. Look closely at any lists of points numbered 1, 2, 3, etc. Be sure you know why the authors have included whatever charts, maps, and pictures there are. Go over any questions and exercises at the end of the chapter; they usually stress the main ideas.

7. *Pause after each paragraph or section of the book to see if you can recall the main ideas.* If you cannot, reread the passage. This pausing for recall and review is one of the best ways to fix the ideas in your mind. (Of course, you don't do this if you are reading a novel or story, for that is quite a different activity from reading for mastery of facts.)

8. *Mark your book if you own it.* Reading should be an active

process. Don't just sit back and let the words come in your eyes and be absorbed into a sort of mental fog. Instead, read with a pencil in hand and make circles, underlinings, squiggles, etc., to emphasize the main points.

9. *Look up new words if you need to.* Always keep a dictionary at your place of study. After you've looked up a word, try to use it a couple of times in the next day or so to implant it in your mind. However, don't do so much looking up that it breaks the train of thought of the passage.

10. *When you've finished an assignment, think back and try to recall the main ideas.* This is a quick way to fix the ideas in your mind and to show where you need to reread. Don't just heave a sigh of relief and close the book when you reach the last word. Try to answer any end-of-chapter questions. If you cannot, review the appropriate section.

11. *Remember, there are different kinds of reading for different kinds of assignments.* Get your mind set for the kind of reading you think applies:

a. Skimming — to get a general overview of the material or to locate a specific item of information.

b. Rapid, relaxed reading — to enjoy a story or an account of something you are interested in.

c. Close, active reading — for mastery, used with textbooks, encyclopedias, and other materials from which you must learn the main facts and ideas.

d. Word-for-word reading (perhaps aloud) — for directions or for math and science problems.

e. Poetry reading (best aloud) — for levels of meaning, metaphor, feeling, sound.

12. *Note and study all corrections and suggestions made to you in class and on your papers.* If your teacher makes a correction on your paper or a suggestion to you in class, that's important. You may well be tested on it later, and you know it's something directed at you that the teacher thinks you particularly need. Don't let it pass. Note also any suggestions made to the class in general. If the teacher thinks something is worth taking the time to mention specially, it's probably important, and teachers have a way of emphasizing in class what they are likely to give tests on later. (Keep a notebook open and pencil available all the time in class.) You don't have to agree with teachers' suggestions, corrections, or opinions of what's important, but it's wise to try to understand their thinking as well as you can.

13. *Plan your time if you have a long-term assignment.* For

instance, if you have three weeks to do a report on a large subject, divide up your time, perhaps spending a week doing rough organization and collecting materials, another week reading the materials and taking notes, and a third week reorganizing and then writing up your report and proofreading it. Don't put off the work until the last few days. You may find yourself without material and without time to search for it.

14. *When doing an assignment, note down any points on which you aren't clear* and raise them in class at the beginning of the next period. This is not only a good way to learn; it also makes a wonderful impression on teachers.

15. *Learn to make a rough outline,* a most valuable tool for organizing your ideas or reviewing materials you have studied. If your teachers have not taught you how to do this, you can find a section on outlining in almost any English textbook. However, it's a waste of time to spend hours making a perfectly formed outline for an ordinary assignment or review. The important thing is to get the main ideas and sub-ideas briefly stated and arranged logically.

16. *When you review for tests, don't reread all the materials.* Instead, use the study aids in the book, the marks you have made, and any notes you have taken on your reading or on what the teacher has emphasized. *Spend your time on the parts you don't know.*

17. *Your basic obligation to your work is to be interested in it.* Try not to set up a block between you and your education by crying, "I'm bored!" or "It's stupid!" You have a perfect right to feel that way, but if you let the feeling control your actions, you may fail to learn. Instead, require yourself to find something in the work that can catch your interest.

Using these seventeen points in studying will take a little more time when you first go over your material, but the total amount of time taken will be less, and your mastery of the work will be more efficient. Of course, if you have a system of your own that you think works better than this one, and you are doing well in school, ignore these suggestions and go on using your own system.

Study habits we call "odd"

There is a danger that we as teachers will impose on our students our own ideas of the right and proper way to learn and do schoolwork, only to find that it simply goes against the nature of some of them. Many people don't learn systematically, step by step, with a plan, at a steady pace. Let's look at several kinds of students who may do well in school, but in their own "peculiar" ways.

The slow shifter is the student who requires considerable time to warm up to a task and get involved in it but who, when involved, progresses powerfully through the task and hates to stop until it's done. He doesn't want to break for supper, he may want to stay up way past his bedtime — until finished. He doesn't like to jump from bit to bit and is slow to shift away from whatever task involves him.

The moody worker sometimes feels like doing homework and sometimes doesn't. The currents of mood run deep and cause what seem like sea changes. When the waters are right for joking or dreaming or talking or sleeping, he will joke, dream, talk, or sleep, and when they are right for working he will outwork anyone else. This student often does poorly in scheduled study halls.

The physical learner is one for whom a desk and chair are a prison, one who reads best while pacing, one who writes in a burst and then takes a turn around the room or downstairs or around the house, and then comes back to burst again.

The talker is the student who, if he has to read something to master it, wants to talk about it, argue about it, say what he thinks, find out what others think. He'll bother his parents or brothers and sisters with talk or spend much of his homework time on the telephone. His mind is turned on and his thinking stimulated by verbal exchange. By this means he learns well. Without it, he languishes.

The slow learner is not stupid but needs plenty of time to assimilate material and to accomplish his work. He may do well, even brilliantly, but he can't do it fast. Often he is thorough, sometimes he argues with and thinks about the book (or the test item) as he goes. He just can't be rushed. If he is, he doesn't finish or finishes poorly. (A survey of Phi Beta Kappa members showed that those students who excel academically tend to be rather slow readers.) Teachers and parents err seriously when they equate slow with dull or stupid and when they equate speed with intelligence. Very often the brightest students will take the longest time to do a piece of homework that involves creativity because they are aware, as a less able student would not be, of the many possibilities it offers for interesting accomplishment and pleasure.

The last-minute artist is the student, so annoying to any plodder, who gets the assignment and then goes apparently carefree until the last moment, when, after an all-night orgy of reading and writing, the paper that took most people three weeks to do is produced in what seems little more than a trice. It is always hard not to look at such papers with a hostile and resentful eye. I have to force myself to read and evaluate each paper for what it is, not for how is was prepared.

The buckler under pressure gets all nervous if he's hurried. He likes to have work assigned well in advance and to proceed systematically until it's done — often well before it's due, never late. He buckles mentally and does poorly if hurried.

The cramped-hand kid finds the act of writing slow torture. He should be taught to type. He may also do better if allowed to give up cursive writing and go back to "printing" separate letters. After a few days of practice, the change to printing eases and speeds up the handwriting of this kind of student.

Therefore, while we must instruct our students in study and mastery techniques, we must be careful never to force them into a style of learning that is contrary to their natures. If we do, some of our students could fail, do less well, and even develop a much poorer opinion of themselves than necessary.

A good approach is to say, "Here are some study skills that work well for many people. If they work for you, fine. If they don't, then make your own system. If you have trouble doing that, we'll talk about it." It is also reassuring to describe some of the successful "different" (a better word than "odd") styles given above. Any students who recognize themselves in one or more of them can say, "Wow, that's me!" and feel much better.

Young students, and their parents, tend to have such reverence for standard study habits solemnly pronounced by the teacher that they will go to damaging lengths to conform or require their children to conform. If a student is having trouble doing his independent work, try to find time to confer with him and his parents. Find out exactly how he goes about the job, what causes him trouble, and help him figure out a way that will work for him.

10.
Homework

Hint 56. Studies should be adapted to the capacity of the pupils.   *Abbie G. Hall*

Many conscientious parents and teachers seem to feel that homework, like the poor, "you have always with you" — or ought to. It seems to be, as one parent observed, "a thing kids don't have any of when it's time for their favorite TV program but lots of when it's time for bed."

One real problem with homework is the mindlessness with which so much of it can be done. A student, when asked by his parents to turn off the radio while doing his homework, said, "But I have to have something to keep my mind on while I'm doing my homework."

Why homework?

At its best, homework grows out of ongoing interest and work. It should not be a dose prescribed against idleness but a vital extension of learning begun at school. "Homework" really is a misnomer. "Independent work," or "directed independent study," are better terms. This work, much of which may be done at home, can serve one or more of the following four purposes: (1) to give the student a chance to practice and master skills or content taught at school; (2) to encourage or require independent creativity, such as writing, projects, research, crafts, or art; (3) to encourage or require wide independent reading; (4) to provide time for reading "study" material in courses like history.

Never let your teaching plan fall into a pattern of having

students do most of their learning at home and using class time for recitation (a sterile and boring activity) or testing. Too often teachers simply say, "All right, for tomorrow learn the material on pages 37-52 and write a one-page essay on it." In such a situation, who is doing the teaching? It's the parents, or the poor students, struggling alone or together on the telephone, teaching themselves. Too often little real teaching gets done at all, and very little learning occurs, except learning to feel frustrated.

Preteaching

When you assign specific homework, it helps greatly if you anticipate problems and difficulties students are likely to have with it, and then preteach, that is, teach students what they need to know to do the assignment well, rather than having it be an exercise in making mistakes and reinforcing bad habits.

Too many of us say to our students, in effect, "Here's the assignment; now go do it." Then, when the time comes to read and mark it, we are surprised and discouraged by the poor quality of the work, by how many people made mistakes they shouldn't have made, by how many failed to see or take advantage of seemingly obvious possibilities for creativity, or even by the sad fact that some students couldn't do the assignment at all — or chose not to. You think you're discouraged, but probably the students are even more discouraged. After all, it is they, not you, who have failed to perform well and whose work is being evaluated.

Of course, students can learn some important lessons from their mistakes, and a post mortem can show them how to do better next time. Even so, it is much easier for them and for you if you figure out in advance what the difficulties, problems, and simple mistakes are likely to be and then teach how to deal with them. That way, students get practice in doing things right, not wrong, and they feel good, not bad, about their work when they hand it in and when you hand it back. And it saves you the time and misery of correcting the same mistakes on paper after paper.

So before turning students loose on an assignment, try to show them how to do what's needed to succeed. You can do this in two phases. I'll use a typical writing assignment as an example.

1. *Let the students ask.* Take time to ask the students what problems they think they are likely to have in doing the assignment and then discuss and instruct as necessary. Here are some of the questions they might ask.

"What do I write about?" Suggest a specific topic or two, ask others in the class to make suggestions, and offer to confer later with anyone who is really stuck.

"Where do I get the information I'll need?" Again, discuss and suggest. One source students often ignore is their own ideas and experience or those of people they know.

"How long does it have to be?" Avoid setting an exact length unless you're working on the discipline of strictly limiting one's writing to 50-100 words as part of the assignment. Whatever the length, always stress that what is said is more important than how long it is.

"How do I get started? I always have trouble starting." Suggest that students just begin to write freely — even if what they first write later turns out to be the middle of the paper — without editing or worrying. Then they can go over what they've written and rearrange it, if need be. Or they can simply write about an important fact or two and add a few sentences on their significance. Remind them that most serious writers throw away a lot of what they've written once they get going.

"How will the assignment be graded?" Will you give one mark, or several? Will you comment on it? Explain exactly what your plan is and ask whether it seems fair. Tell how you are going to evaluate content — quality, quantity, relevance, organization, etc. — spelling, punctuation, and so forth. (See Chapter 23, "Dealing with the Written Work of Students.")

"Will our papers be read aloud to the class?" Tell your thoughts on the subject and ask the class how it feels, but don't necessarily be limited by the answers you get. Some people benefit by having their work shared, even though they don't request it. Discuss who the audience for the paper is — the teacher? the class? others?

2. *Teach the students.* Even after all questions have been discussed, there still may be things that need to be taught before the assignment is done. You should have thought

through the assignment in advance and even done it yourself (the best way to reveal booby traps), noting any problems that might crop up. Here are a few typical ones.

Spelling. If you foresee any familiar troublemakers on the horizon, write them on the board and quickly point out the problems. If the students are writing about an "embarrassing" experience, discuss the two *a*'s, double *r*, and double *s*. A description of "character" involves *ch*, two *a*'s, and *er*. And so on.

Mechanics. If the assignment involves written dialogue, remind the class of the rules for paragraphing and punctuating it. You can even have the students copy a sample from the board, if you think that might help.

Organization. Many writing assignments involve essays, which require arranging several ideas in some coherent order and subordinating topics and subtopics convincingly. This skill needs to be taught again and again because some students are slow to learn it, others are quick to forget — or ignore — it. A straight-out lesson or two can be useful, either for the entire class or for the few who especially need it.

Sentence variety. If the assignment involves describing a series of actions or steps, some students may well write their narratives as a series of short sentences that each begin with, "Then . . ." These students need to be reminded of the importance of varied structure and length for sentences. A few pairs of "Then" and revised "Then" sentences on the board can be useful here.

Selecting and developing. Many immature writers, faced with telling an experience or writing a story, tend to plod on and on, giving each thought equal weight. Students need to be shown how to cut passages that add no interest (what the family had for breakfast the morning Mike almost got killed falling into a quarry) but to develop in precise detail the interesting parts (Mike's feelings and what he heard and saw just before and just after he fell).

Title and beginning. Many students do not give enough attention to the way their paper begins or to its title. A few good and bad examples can help them keep these matters in mind.

First and second drafts and revisions. You may need to remind some students of the value of writing a first draft, then reading it *aloud* and making revisions — a single word here, a sentence there, order, emphasis, beginning and ending, or whatever else doesn't sound right and interesting. Hand out a dittoed sheet for the class to revise together as you and they think aloud about it. Urge students to be highly critical strangers to their own work, to get outside it and be hard on it.

Proofreading. Make it clear whether you accept crossed-out and correc ed words or whether you require a completely neat copy. I happen to think that it's a discouraging waste of time for students to copy a page over just because they've made a few errors that can be plainly fixed.

Schedule. When making any assignment, but especially a long one, discuss the timetable for completing it. As a useful form of preteaching, you can suggest (or require) that the work be shown to you at various stages — notes, then a preliminary outline, then a first draft, and so on. If several students run into problems at any one stage, you may see the need for discussion or instruction for a few or all students.

One last word about preteaching: sometimes it is hard to judge whether you have done too much of it. If you foresee and deal with every possible problem, you may find yourself taking the joy of discovery out of the assignment. Remember, some mistakes are worth making just for the lessons that they teach. Sometimes it is best to allow students, especially able and highly motivated ones, to rush forth and err and learn thus not to err again.

Another danger, especially with timid and academically weak students, is to load an assignment with so many cautions and pitfall warnings that the students become paralyzed. Yet another possibility is to preteach to the point of boredom. Preteach in bits, and only in the bits essential to the matter at hand. It is better to let enthusiastic students fling themselves into an assignment while they're still excited and deal with problems afterwards than to try to ensure dead uniformity and competence in advance.

Making the purpose of homework clear

When students ask, "Why do we have to do this? I don't see the point," we too often answer, "Because it will help you," or

"Because you should do your homework," or "Because I say so." So the students, if they're dutiful, go through the motions with no understanding of what they're doing and how it fits into a larger objective worth accomplishing.

Instead, we should stay alert to ways of showing why the work is important and worth doing — even if the reward is somewhat removed in time. We need to keep on cultivating an understanding of the larger context in which specific pieces of work are done. A sense of context can have enormous influence on learning and morale.

It is not enough that we have a grand scheme in our own minds; it must be in the minds of our students, too. When someone asks, "Why do we have to do this?" turn the question to the class and let them discuss it until they see why. Sometimes it is useful to say, "If you aren't convinced that this is worth doing, then you don't have to do it — but you've got to let me try to convince you before you say no."

Some suggestions about homework

While some of the following suggestions may seem fairly obvious, keeping them in mind can make life easier for you and your students in the long run.

● Don't require perfect neatness on practice exercises. Many school tasks are not worth doing neatly — or even well.

● Always put written assignments in the same place — either the same place on the board, for short ones, or the same place in the room, for more complicated assignments that have been dittoed and distributed but have been mislaid by some students.

● Keep in touch with other teachers so that too many of you don't load on lots of work or tests at the same time. Listen to your students; they'll let you know when this happens.

● Never use homework as a punishment.

● Try to assign homework a week or more at a time, with due dates noted, so that students can learn to plan their time and take advantage of slack time in one subject to work on another.

● Accept good excuses for homework not done — but not too many. Students often have legitimate reasons for not getting their work done, and you should recognize them.

- Allow for a range of responses in as many assignments as possible to challenge able students while allowing the less able to find some degree of success in their work.

Contracts

In some schools, long-term independent work is done according to a contract system, which can be used for students in grade 5 and up. A contract is simply a signed agreement between student and teacher whereby the student is to accomplish a certain task or amount of work in a given subject by a certain time.

Contracts are a good way of getting students involved in making decisions about their own work and how they are going to do it. They are also a good device for tailoring work to individual students' interests and capacities. If your classroom is well furnished with materials and has a cooperative atmosphere, contracts can put students on their own while you spend time on individual instruction.

The terms of a simple contract (which starts out by naming the student, the teacher, the work to be accomplished, and the date the work is to be completed) are these: (1) reading to be done, (2) other investigation to be done, (3) writing to be done, (4) hoped-for benefits from completing the contract, and (5) how contracted work will be evaluated or graded.

The common custom of "negotiating" the terms of a contract may put an element of contest or opposition (teacher vs. student) into the work situation. It is probably a better idea to discuss and agree on terms. Otherwise, the whole business can turn out to be more of a con than a contract, more a device to get more work out of students than an agreement willingly arrived at.

Sometimes a contract may seem reasonable at first but later turn out to be too hard or not challenging enough. Since contracts are good only if students can complete them with reasonable diligence, their terms should always be open to change. Mistakes in judgment, if discussed and rectified, can be good learning opportunities. Periodic progress checks between student and teacher are desirable so that any problems can be spotted and dealt with before they get out of hand.

It usually works best if only part of class time is spent on contract work. Students like to know what times they will be doing contract work and when they will be doing other kinds of work. Contract work can spill over into homework, of course, and some enthusiastic students may do it entirely on their own.

Independent projects

An independent project, also adaptable to students from grade 5 on up, differs from a contract only in degree. With older students in a flexible school, such a project may even involve being allowed to leave school one day a week or for certain periods on certain days.

Independent projects that fail usually do so because they are vaguely defined, with no clear notion of how they are to be carried out or evaluated, and because they are not carefully and regularly monitored. Some of the comments about contracts apply here, too.

As for monitoring, a definite, written timetable for checking progress and phases of accomplishment works best. Let's take a six-week project as an example. You draw up a simple form entitled, say, "Periodic Progress Report." Each Friday, for six Fridays, in the space allotted, the student rates himself according to one of the following statements: (1) "I am doing well, am on schedule, have no problems," (2) "I am making progress but need to discuss," (3) "I have real problems and may have to shift projects," (4) "I have nearly finished my project," or (5) "Other (describe)." If need be, the student adds an explanation. The following Monday, the teacher returns the form, with written comment, and sets up a conference, if necessary. In this way, the student is not left on his own, possibly to flounder or fail.

Homework and parents

Teachers are often asked by parents how much they should get involved in their children's homework. In general, we can ask them to do the following things.

- If you can, provide good conditions for study — the needed space, equipment, and quiet time.
- Don't forget, it's independent work, so be sure your child

does it independently. If he can't do it, tell him to ask the teacher.

● Never do homework for your child. This teaches the child very little and is only likely to hide from teachers what they have to know about weakness or lack of understanding so that they can teach what is needed. In other words, never shield your child from the legitimate consequences of not doing his job, whether because of laziness, boredom, or inability to do it. If there are no consequences when you feel there should be, ask for a conference with the teacher.

● Be a source of information, if you can, or put your child in touch with sources of information (library, books at home).

● If you can straighten out a simple matter of fact or misunderstanding with a little teaching of your own, go ahead, but be careful not to teach too much or teach a trick that shortcuts understanding. (This is especially likely to happen in math, where answer-getting tricks work up to a point but not beyond.)

● Don't insist that your child have work to do at home. Many students get their homework done in free periods at school.

● There are many styles of learning. Don't expect your child to use the same ones you do.

● It's OK for students to consult about homework on the telephone — often one of the best ways to learn — provided that (1) they are really exchanging ideas, not answers, (2) one isn't imposing on the good will and intelligence of the other, and (3) the rest of the family isn't being kept off the phone.

● In general, parents get too involved in homework. There's enough friction at home without adding homework to the list of causes.

11.
Organizing and
Managing the People

In this chapter, I want to talk about organizing and managing the people with whom a teacher has to deal. Then, in the next three chapters, I offer some ideas for organizing the place, the materials, and time. These cannot, of course, be separated in your classroom, for everything affects everything else.

"Defending walls"

The 1960's saw a strong anti-wall movement among school people. Everything was supposed to be open. When I think of walls, I think of Robert Frost's poem "Mending Wall," which begins, "Something there is that doesn't love a wall," and tells about Frost's fence-loving neighbor, reciting his litany, "Good fences make good neighbors." One could write a parody of Frost's poem and call it "Defending Walls," starting with, "Something there is necessitates four walls," and ending, "Walled classrooms help good learning."

I am far from alone in believing in walls. A friend of mine, first a brilliant English teacher and now in charge of innovative programs in a large school district, says that it is in the very nature of people and spaces that students and teachers should be brought together in schools in a ratio of about 25 to 1, enclosed by four classroom walls.

Why? That group of twenty-five is about the largest one in which people can view one another as a group, talk among themselves in a social voice (as distinguished from an intimate

or a public voice), and move and pass things around quickly. A group larger than that is too public to work well, and a smaller group makes inefficient use of a skilled teacher's time and salary in most schools, even though some prosperous public schools and most independent schools have classes of twenty or less.

We know that a lot of excellent teaching went on in one-room schoolhouses, like Abbie Hall's, where students of all ages came together for interdisciplinary learning, perhaps with more emphasis on the "disciplinary" than on the "inter."

Similarly, we know how much planning, caring, intelligence, vision, and money were invested during the last couple of decades to create "open" schools, "open" classrooms, and large, barrier-free open spaces to permit all possible combinations of methods and people teaching and learning.

Now, however, the four-walls order of things seems gradually yet certainly to be re-establishing itself. I think this has come about because teachers, students, and communities find that four-walled classrooms full of students with teachers teaching subjects work best. "Tear down the walls" has become "Build back the walls," with demands in many schools and communities that those expensive, carefully planned opennesses be partitioned off so that schoolwork can be organized, discussed, and supervised within manageable units of space.

Since at least 90 per cent of all students and teachers are grouped for schoolwork in classrooms, and since my own experience convinces me that this is usually the best way, my suggestions here are based on the prevailing pattern of school organization. They are open to whatever alterations the ingenious reader might wish to make.

A word about "open"

For some people, "open" means all the good things that are the opposite of "closed": flexibility, individual attention, willingness to accept new ideas, developing students' ability to make choices and become responsible for their own learning. For others, "open" means all the bad things that go with laxity: planlessness, freedom to wander unwatched, no attention to basics, and a naive faith that children, if surrounded by an all-forgiving pleasantness and absence of requirements, will somehow stumble across learning.

In fact, in a "traditional" classroom, if the teaching is competent and the materials good, there is much individual attention and openness; and in an "innovative" open classroom, if the teaching is competent, one finds careful structure, planning, and close attention to the essentials of learning for each student.

Perhaps the greatest misconception about open schools and classrooms is that they are unplanned. In reality, it takes excellent teachers and very careful planning to manage a good open school or classroom. So enough of using "open" and "traditional" as opposites. They aren't, not at all.

Some elements of organization

Organization and management — or lack of them — originate within each person. Our purpose as teachers should be to help each student become a more organized, self-managed person, even if only gradually and never uniformly. Some of our students will never achieve this goal, while others will have achieved it before we ever meet them. Meanwhile, our job is to see that we and our students can live and learn together.

The simplest, most common way to organize and manage a class is as a single group, with everyone expected to do the same work at the same time. It is possible to combine a great deal of individual work with an all-class approach if you are skillful in the way you make and deal with assignments.

You can modify the whole-class approach by breaking the group up into smaller groups or having all students work on their own. The best cues to the pros and cons of any method of grouping come from the needs of your students, the requirements of your school, and your own abilities, training, personality, and temperament. Here are some ideas to keep in mind, no matter what methods you use.

1. *Monitoring.* You, as the teacher, are responsible for monitoring — for keeping track of — the academic, social, psychological, and physical situation of each student. You hear what students say or don't say. You read and deal with what

students write and keep a record of it. You see what they are reading. You find ways for them to record and share with you their progress and problems. You know where their bodies — if not their minds — are, or are supposed to be, at all times. You do your best to see who is bored and who is overchallenged. And you give tests to keep track of who is falling behind and who needs special help.

A careful system of monitoring is especially important in a classroom where students work on their own most of the time, because it is so easy for students to go out to pasture. See Chapters 17 and 24 for suggested types of monitoring.

2. *Groups.* Students like to work in groups as a change from always meeting as a single class. Elementary teachers have long been expert at making and managing groups, especially to teach reading. Most subjects lend themselves to differentiated homework and reading and writing assignments, making it possible to avoid straight ability grouping and the bad effects it can have.

In subjects involving sequential skills (foreign language, math), ability grouping is probably necessary unless the work is mostly individual. In such cases, the bad effects of ability grouping can be reduced by allowing for elective units, which makes it possible to mix people of varying abilities in the same courses or units.

Here are some ways to set up groups with frequently changing membership.

Random groups. Say you want five groups of five. Just count "1-2-3-4-5" around the room and tell each group number where to meet.

Interest groups. If your room is arranged in interest centers (see Chapter 12), let students sign up for their interests and needs, listing three in order of preference, and then set up groups of similar sizes. Later, when new groups are formed, those who didn't get first choice before should now be given preference.

Named groups. Younger students enjoy belonging to a group with a name (let them make up names or choose colors) or groups that temporarily call themselves villages or tribes or teams.

Editing and correcting groups. These can be groups of

three, or even just pairs, to deal with one another's written work or other work before it gets handed in or shown to the class. You can count these groups off in such a way that best friends and habitual sitters together can be separated.

Discussion panel. In preparing for an assignment, it can sometimes help to have a panel of students to discuss the subject and stir up ideas. After the panel has talked for about five minutes, you can open the discussion to the whole class, with you presiding.

Dispersal groups. If you have a stable class population, it saves time to form groups in advance, seeing to it that each group has some able people in it and someone who can act as chairman. Make a list of these groups so that when you say, "Disperse," the class can go quickly into small-group work. This plan works well for discussion, brainstorming, sharing writing, and other work that needs a small audience.

"Sides." A classic but poor method for organizing a class into teams is to have two captains "choose up sides." This makes some children feel rejected as the pool of the unchosen dwindles. Far better to use the random system.

3. *Panel of experts.* Most classes have students who are especially good at certain parts of the work. Since time is always short for you to work individually with students, you can have "experts" in spelling, fractions, research techniques, working with clay, and so forth, chosen by you, by the class, or by themselves as volunteers. Post their names so that people will know whom to see when the time comes. You will need to keep an eye on things to be sure that the "experts" have expertise and that they aren't just showing off, being dictators, or simply goofing off with a friend.

4. *Always something to do.* In any classroom not entirely dominated by up-front teaching, there are inevitably times when students run out of things to do and find themselves at loose ends. While sitting around doing nothing, chatting, and looking out the window aren't terrible, it's still a good idea to have something ready for anyone who runs out of work, like a quotation, topic, or assignment for "extra credit" in a special place in the room, preferably changed each day; or a series of "job boxes," from which students can pick out a piece of work and do it; or a long-term assignment to be done independently.

5. *Silence bell.* Sometimes, when the class is working in

groups, you need a quick way to lower the noise or to get complete quiet. Shouting over the class just makes things worse and everyone nervous. Much more neutral is a bell, with one ding for "Lower the decibels" and two dings for "Quiet, please; I have something to say." But use the bell sparingly.

6. *Volunteer assistants.* Many teachers are greatly helped by volunteer assistants. They may be parents (preferably not of children in the class), older students (at least three grades older), or people from the community. Some men and women, wondering whether they really want to teach, need a way to find out whether they have the temperament and the touch. Able, experienced teachers who have left full-time teaching for other responsibilities may still have time to do some teaching. Such people can be a tremendous asset to full-time teachers and their classes, even (or especially) if they have greater skill and experience than the teacher with whom they are working. Another good resource is retired people, some of whom possess ample skills and experience.

Arrangements with volunteers — assistants, apprentices, aides — work best if certain guidelines are followed. Volunteers should commit themselves to a definite schedule. "I'll come when I can" usually doesn't work, except for tasks that can be done at any time, like sorting materials, making signs, or filing records. Take time at the beginning to explain fully what your plans are and what part the volunteer will play in them.

Because volunteers expect to get as much from the experience as they give, you need to spend some time with them regularly and, when special needs arise, to plan and talk. Volunteers should not just be given routine tasks and dirty work. And they should pitch in almost right away, not spend the first few days just observing.

Volunteers provide extra help — hands, eyes, ears, minds — for you and your students. They can help individual students, work with groups, make presentations to the entire class, teach a unit, read and evaluate papers, and do whatever else is needed. It is up to you to let them know in advance about various routines — how you go about reading and evaluating papers, for instance — and give them whatever practice they need.

Volunteers should understand that you are in charge. Plan

to sit down after a week or two to talk about how things are going. Not all teams work out; whether yours is working or not is your decision. Volunteers need praise and encouragement, just like the rest of us. Never take volunteers for granted. Find out what they do best and feature that.

Volunteers can be excellent critics of your work, if you ask them to be and are secure enough to take what they say and benefit from it. Volunteers should understand that they are working as professionals and thus that whatever goes on in the classroom stays in the classroom and in the school, and is not a topic of social conversation. Finally, volunteers need to be monitored, just as students are, by you.

7. *Students teaching students.* Students can teach classmates or they can teach students in other grades. Younger students tend to learn a great deal when slightly older students teach them, partly because they receive the "teacher's" total attention, and partly because they feel much freer to ask one other person questions than they do an entire class. Perhaps it is the student teachers who learn the most. When they know they're going to have to teach something, they know they have to learn it themselves.

12.
Organizing the Place

> *Hint 27.* Choose certain places on your
> blackboard for certain lessons, and, by
> habitually following this rule, the children will
> come to know where to look for instructions
> as to each lesson.   *Abbie G. Hall*

In this chapter, I am assuming that your classroom is large enough to permit some variety of arrangement and that the chairs and desks are not bolted to the floor in rows. But even if your room is utterly filled with rows, and each row with students, with the overflow sitting on the window sills, skim this chapter quickly for an idea or two about using walls and crannies and then go on to the next chapter.

Ideas that work well

It is a good idea to set your room up as attractively and workably as you can well before your first class meets in the fall. Once a physical order is established, the class can talk and write about it and decide what to do with it — "What is the best way to arrange students, teacher, and furniture?" "How can we fix our room up better?"

You can draw various seating arrangements on the board — circle, square, clusters, rows — and ask the students to talk about the advantages and disadvantages of each scheme, depending on various situations. Even if you don't want to have the class discuss these questions, put them to yourself and ask other teachers what they think. Constructive as it may be to ask students and other teachers about arranging and equipping your classroom, however, you are the one who has to live in it and with it. Respect your own needs; you are the one who is there all day, day in and day out.

Which of the following suggestions you can and want to use depends on the size of your room, class, and budget, the kind of school you're in, and the kind of person you are, among other things. Some things that seem suitable only for elementary school may surprise you when you try them out on older students, who spend far too much time in dull, sloppy classrooms, as far as I have observed.

1. *Special spots.* Having some special spots in the room can be a way to save time and avoid useless talk. Others can help you make use of free space in unexpected places.

Homework. Have a special place on the board where homework assignments are always written.

"Look here first." Some teachers find it fun to have classes always look in a certain place the minute they come in the room for a quotation they can discuss, an exercise to do before class starts, a joke, or a surprise.

Word list. If the class is working on something that involves special vocabulary, or if interesting words come up, have a special place for writing these words (with short definitions) so that everyone can see them and leave them up for a few days. Every couple of weeks you can give a multiple-choice test on these words, with extra credit for those who do well. Students can submit items to be included on the test.

Hand-in slot or box. If you have a slot or box, students don't have to hunt for you in order to turn in papers or other written work. Check the box every day before you go home.

Message and hand-back envelope. Make a file holder or large envelope for each student, with the name clearly marked, that you can tack up on the wall or file in an open box. You can use these envelopes for returning papers, making special assignments, or passing on other messages.

Bulletin boards. Most classrooms have bulletin boards, but usually not enough, and almost always dull looking. Besides being a stimulus for activities and projects, bulletin boards can reward good, interesting work by displaying it for all to see and admire. Have a contest to see who comes up with the best ideas for livening up your bulletin boards.

The upper reaches. Many classrooms ignore the three feet of wall just below the ceiling. Install bulletin board material in the space, and you'll see how many decorative and instructional things it will hold.

2. *Special centers.* In most schools, the center of each classroom is the classroom itself. Think about setting up various centers within the room, setting them off from one another by bookcases, movable shelves or partitions, filing cabinets, or sofas. You can also make a center by arranging chairs or desks around a table or carpet. Corners are good places, too, especially in old buildings, which have a lot of them. What may seem like a cramped, dusty nook may, with a little fixing up, be just the place for a student or two to learn best.

Learning centers or stations. Learning centers have tables, seats, and bins, files, and shelves for materials on various projects and assignments. Students may go there when they don't have to be doing something else, or you may prefer to work out a progression from learning center to learning center as the basic daily schedule for each student. It's a good idea to have some rules about how many students may be in a certain center at a given time and what they may and may not do there. In *Law and Order in Grade 6-E* (Boston: Little, Brown, 1972), Kim Marshall tells in a most practical manner about the learning station method of teaching he developed.

Interest centers. Similar to learning centers, these focus on a special interest or theme. One example: the themes of the various chapters of the textbook the class is using can form the subjects for interest centers.

Carrels. Carrels are walled-in spaces for individual work, each having a chair, a desktop, and a shelf above for books. Some are movable. A carrel gives the student psychological privacy and increased ability to concentrate right in the classroom. Some schools have carrels left over from the heyday of language labs. Look around to see if any are tucked away in your school.

Lofts. Lofts — two-story, roughly made, semi-open rooms — have the appeal of a treehouse for younger grades all the way through eighth grade. In them, students may work, read, talk, and relax. Planning and building a loft is a good cooperative project for the class, the shop class, and others in the school.

The teacher's desk. Your desk is probably the most important spot in the room, so you should think about making it easy and comfortable to talk with you there. Some teachers put a couple of special chairs near their desks, partially set off from the common gaze, where students can feel easy talking. A small table helps, too, if you're going to be looking at written work. A sign-up list on the board keeps students from having to wait in line to see you.

Classroom library. Although the school library is of immense value for teaching and learning, it is elsewhere. For some students that is a major obstacle, for others a pleasure. If you can collect some books in your own classroom and work out a simple system for borrowing and return, students will do much more reading and looking up than if they have to go to the library. Some students may donate books, and your school may have money available for classroom collections. Think about moving some of the books around from time to time to catch attention. For some reason, moving books around stimulates their use. A revolving exhibit of three or four books on the chalk rail of the blackboard is simple and works as well as anything.

Paperback bookstore. A small place to buy or order paperbacks is a wonderful way of getting students reading and writing. If you buy a book, you're likely to read it. Your school librarian should be able to tell you which paperback publishers and local distributors are most helpful and convenient.

Book exchange or sale. Students who wish to give books away can put them on a "free" shelf, and those who want to sell them can put them on a "for sale" shelf. Such a barter and small-change economy may involve some record keeping (which often can be delegated to students), but it stimulates reading, writing, and conversation.

3. *Furniture.* This book is not the place for a treatise on classroom furniture, but here are a few suggestions.

A place of one's own. Most students like to have a place they can call their own and where they can store things. There is much to be said for the old-fashioned classroom desk with the storage space under the lid. If necessary, the lids can be equipped with combination locks, which is much cheaper than having lockers.

Donated furniture. Don't forget the possibility of donated furniture, if your school doesn't have regulations against it. A few easy chairs, bureaus, cabinets, a couch or two, and rugs and carpets can often be found among school families or at yard sales, second-hand stores, and rummage sales.

Old school furniture. Be sure to explore the basement and

storage areas of your school to look for good old furniture that has been displaced. The old and worn, which often has far more appeal than the new, can provide variety and stimulation and comfort.

4. *Signs and labels.* Liberal use of signs is an obvious necessity in rooms where children are still learning to read and build their vocabularies. Names of places, directions, rules, shelf labels, jokes, quotations, and anything else of interest can be printed by you and by the students on large sheets of paper or tagboard for the reading, enlightenment, and amusement of all.

5. *Visitors.* Some schools and classes make elaborate preparations for visitors — a map of the room, a sheet explaining what goes on and pointing out features the visitor might look for — and others do very little. Here are some of the items that might be on the handout sheet (adapted from "What's Going on Here?" by John Harkins, *Studies in Education,* Germantown Friends School, Philadelphia, Pa., fall 1975).

To Visitors

Welcome to Room XX!

Please take a seat in the corner and look around our room. See if you can figure out why things are arranged as they are. The key words are: *independence, creativity,* and *individualization.*

What evidence can you see of the following? Who is actively (perhaps quietly) involved in learning? How do you know?

Is the teacher dipping the spoon into the pot of knowledge and feeding it to the students, or are students feeding themselves?

Is there a schedule anywhere in the room?

Do students proceed on their own from task to task, or does the teacher dominate?

Where do students go when they have a problem?

When and why does the teacher intervene?

What evidence of creative activity of students can you see in the room? Is any on display?

If you quietly ask a student to explain something in the room that you do not understand, can he or she do it?

In general, especially in many-centered, "open" classrooms, it helps to have a few students who are ready to give any visitor a tour of the room and explain what's what and why. Some students enjoy doing this, it makes a good impression on visitors, and it lets you keep on with your work without making visitors feel ignored.

13.
Selecting, Organizing, and Managing the Materials

Hint 28. Blackboard, crayon, books, pointers, pencils, maps, etc., are the teacher's tools. The convenient and orderly arrangement of these tools will save time and, also, every day teach an object lesson in orderly habits.
Abbie G. Hall

What I write here is affected by my training and experience: I have taught mostly English and social studies; mechanical things tend to grind to a stop and fall apart in my hands; reading gives me more pleasure and information than television and films. I agree with Bruno Bettelheim that "television captures the imagination but does not liberate it [whereas] a good book at once stimulates and frees the mind."

Books

My view is that the most valuable "materials" to use for teaching are books — books read and discussed, mastered and enjoyed, related to the experiences and feelings of students. They are also the best sources of vicarious experience (you don't have to *do* everything to learn it). Further, in this age of devices and machinery, we should not forget that a book is a nearly ideal teaching machine. It is light, portable, attractive, durable, and tough; it covers a vast range of subjects; it is entirely self-pacing, perfect for all teaching methods; and it is cheap, especially if it is a paperback.

These days it is fashionable to be scornful of standard hardcover textbooks, which come in series, last a long time, and often are accompanied by workbooks. Although I'll admit that after the first two or three years of teaching, I have never wanted to stick with a series of workbooks, I believe that a well-organized textbook and its accompaniments is far better

than the chaos that results when an inexperienced teacher tries to be "open" and improvise too much.

Good texts and textbook series are skillfully put together, usually by able teachers and experienced editors. They are geared to individualized instruction, with each student moving at his or her own pace. And there's no question that many published workbooks and prepared ditto masters contain much better exercises than we can devise in the short time most of us have. So don't scorn published materials. Take time at educational conventions to visit the exhibits to see new textbooks and workbooks. But don't neglect old books. A good literature anthology, for example, never goes out of date, and you and your students can use it year after year.

Many publishing companies now provide a marvelous selection of fairly inexpensive paperbacks. They present them in various ways to stimulate individual interest and initiative while offering enough supporting materials (guidebooks, ditto masters, cassettes, posters, etc.) to give good, sound structure and coherence to a class.

Some hard-pressed teachers worry about using more than one textbook or one system of teaching because they can't possibly read and know all the books they might have in their classrooms that their students might use. This doesn't matter as long as you have a general idea of what's available. There are several points to be made in this connection.

• The only books you need to read all the way through and know thoroughly are the ones you expect to teach to the entire group or to refer to very often. Students can help you and their classmates by telling about good new books that they have read. By having students make brief written reports evaluating the books they read, you can quickly find out what they are reading and how they are reacting to it. You might wish to start a "best books" board, a "highly recommended" file, or, as a reverse twist, a "don't read" board.

• Another good idea is to make up quite a long list of books for independent reading for each student in your class, and not just English classes. Sometimes it helps to divide the list into "hard," "average," and "easy" categories. Many teachers require students to read a certain number of books from the list every two weeks or every month, making allowances for those who simply can't read that much or are temporarily preoccupied with other concerns.

• Another way to encourage students to read more is to give each of them an independent reading notebook in which they may keep a record of reading done. Instead of the usual dreary full-length book report, they can note, in this book, the author, title, number of pages, where they found the book, difficulty and enjoyment ratings, brief description, and comment (how the book affected them, to whom they recommend it). This system enables you to evaluate students' reading and to keep in touch with what they are reading so that you can recommend books to others. I believe that independent reading should be an important element of the mark or evaluation students receive for their work.

Other materials

Having acknowledged my preference for books, I must also make some suggestions about other kinds of materials for use in the classroom.

Miscellaneous materials. For lower grades, collect bits of cardboard for word games, piles of paper bags for drawing masks, old socks in which to put things to be felt but not seen and then written about, spring clips for hanging exhibit items to be talked and written about. And so on and on.

Charts of frequently needed facts or ideas. Post large charts around the upper reaches of the room for use as needed. For example, in an English course, charts giving the following information would be useful: the approved form for writing papers and assignments, form for writing plays, grammar symbols, prefixes, suffixes, and roots, spelling rules, poetry terms, characteristics of short stories, principal rules of punctuation. Similar charts for math, science, and social studies are other, obvious possibilities. Having publicly posted information always visible in the room means that the stuff is right there when the students need it, and they can use it to teach or remind themselves without help from anyone else. A chart also enables you to call the attention of the class quickly to a needed item without having to get out books and flip pages.

Individual student folders. It is useful to keep a folder for each student in which you or the student file all the material he or she produces at home or in class after you have dealt with it. You can use this material to show students their progress and accomplishments as well as the areas in which they need to improve. It helps if you keep a master list posted somewhere in the room of each paper and assignment that all students are supposed to have done. Then, from time to time, students can check their folders to be sure that everything that should be there is there.

Extra-credit tests. In a classroom where students work individually a good deal of the time, it is useful to have a supply of extra-credit tests on file and accessible to your students. These tests, which you can buy or make up yourself, should cover whatever areas of the subject you are teaching that can be tested. You can explain to students that if they take and do well on the tests, you will note that fact on their record and give them credit for it. These tests should be available to students to study and practice on at any time before they actually take them. If a test covers worthwhile material, mastering its content before taking the test is a good way to learn. For more on this subject, see Chapter 18.

Special materials and devices

Learning and stimulation can be increased if the classroom is equipped with certain items, provided they are affordable.

Typewriters. A couple of typewriters are a valuable addition to any classroom. Ambitious students can even teach themselves to touch type from a good instruction manual.

Overhead projector and screen. By keeping a projector and screen always in the same place so that you can use them quickly, you can concentrate the attention of the class on a single point as you deal with a paper, an item in a book, a drawing, or a hand-made transparency as the basis of a common lesson. The good old blackboard is more reliable, and it has no bulb to burn out, but the projector is an excellent supplement.

Tape recorder and record player. These devices can stimulate learning in several ways. Students can record and play back to the class a passage, sound effect, or skit as a stimulus for discussion. Recordings of words, music, or both sometimes move students in ways that your voice and theirs cannot. Students who simply cannot get started writing are sometimes helped by talking into a tape recorder and then playing back their talking and copying it. You can quickly tape a special assignment in advance for a student or a group of students, who then listen to the instructions and follow them. (It is strange how sometimes our electronic voice can compel more concentrated attention than our real voice.)

Calendar and maps. A large calendar is an item some classrooms don't have and should. Even more important are two large maps, one of the world (preferably with the United States shown somewhere other than in the center), and one of the United States. A third, detailed map of the school's community is also useful. Maps may seem old-fashioned and schoolroomy, but they are a constant source of reality, stimulation, and orientation to the world. And there's nothing like a map for settling arguments about facts that aren't worth discussing. Maps, by the way, are even more valuable if you have one set that shows only the physical features of the earth, the nation, and the community, and another set that shows only the political features. It is a good lesson to learn that national boundaries are not visible from space. In fact, some large photographs of earth taken from spaceships are good to post near the maps in your room.

Curtain or large folding screen. Both of these are easy to make and should not be expensive. They are useful, but not essential, for skits, acting short scenes of plays, and sound and voice effects without visible clues.

Lectern or rostrum. Anyone who makes speeches knows how convenient it is to have someplace to put your notes, but thousands of students are required to read their papers, deliver their speeches, and make their reports from papers and notes held in shaking hands or put on a table or desk. A solid music stand (not a flimsy folding one) works well, doesn't cost much, and is adjustable. The real world provides lecterns for speakers, so why not the classroom?

Shelves, bins, drawers, and boxes. Containers and places for storing materials and objects are generally associated with the lower grades, but some teachers find that many high school students, too, welcome and enjoy an attractive variety of non-book materials to hold, arrange, count, draw on, discuss, and write about.

Paste, paper, markers, tape, and scissors. These come in handy for students of all ages.

Games. Collect, as budget and resourcefulness allow, as many educational games as you can. Often students are glad to bring in their own. Games are great for filling extra bits of time, for enriching the day of fast finishers, and for bringing students together informally.

I believe that school budgets should allocate to all teachers a certain sum that they can spend, without getting special permission or making out a purchase order, for equipment and materials to improve their work and their classrooms. The money should be meticulously accounted for, of course, and should not be allowed to carry over from one year to the next; each year a fresh sum.

Cleanup and maintenance

Whenever we use a place or thing, we should try to leave it in as good condition as we found it or better. Through class discussion, students can be brought to see the advantage to all if each person does his or her share of the "housekeeping." Tasks can be distributed according to preference and skill, but the aim should be shared responsibility.

Doing one's share offers many opportunities for modest glory and self-esteem. Often the people who are not the most fluent readers, the best speakers, or the most creative poster makers become the best projectionists, book shelvers, bulletin board arrangers, or even sweepers or erasers.

It is worth spending class time on developing good attitudes toward and arrangements for this aspect of school life. Avoid, if possible, the attitude that says, "Well, the janitors will take care of it. After all, it's their job. Our job is the higher, nobler task of education." Bosh.

● And don't assume that all these nice, pleasant ways of organizing are OK for young children but not for adolescents. Schools tend to slide into sloppiness as students get up into seventh and eighth grade, probably because teachers become more concerned with academic work and discipline. These will go better if concern for orderliness continues, not by fiat, but through discussion, agreement, and commitment.

• If possible, try to get this movement going early in the year instead of waiting until things go to pot or you get angry because you have to do it all yourself. Remember, a martyr is someone who has to live with a saint, and we should not expect our students to be martyrs.

Television as a "material"

Television is a material that is impossible to "select, organize, and manage." Its influence in your classroom weighs heavily, and it is largely out of your control. In America, the average home set is on for six and a half hours a day; preschoolers watch 30 to 50 hours a week, spending more than a third of their waking hours before the tube. By graduation, the average high school student will have viewed 18,000 hours of television but attended only 11,000 hours of classroom instruction. These figures are presented by Marie Winn in *The Plug-In Drug* (New York: Bantam Books, 1978), a book I strongly recommend. Winn shows that the damaging effects of television grow out of the process of watching it, not primarily from the poor content of programs. She quotes a mother: "My five-year-old goes into a trance when he watches TV. He just gets locked into what is happening on the screen. He's totally, absolutely absorbed when he watches and oblivious to anything else. If I speak to him when he's watching TV he absolutely doesn't hear me. To get his attention I have to turn the set off. Then he snaps out of it."

The process of watching television for long periods of time is damaging because the programs move at their own fast pace, allowing no time for pause or reflection, no interaction with other minds, no participation, only passive receiving of vigorous, mind-monopolizing stimuli. Television walls its viewers off from their families and from their friends; it can cripple social competence and the ability to discuss, to challenge, or to relate to others intellectually (or in any way except by physical proximity). Its presentations move fast, its images keep shifting as lenses switch and zoom, its content comes in vivid visual splashes reinforced by music, sound effects, and voices, and it totally lacks the left-to-right sequentiality that reading requires. It greatly weakens the capacity to pay attention in class. Its effects are so strong and pervasive that writer and critic Clifton Fadiman sees them as creating what he calls "an alternate life," impervious to traditional classroom teaching.

Of course, defenders of television point out that viewers hear hours of good standard English most of the time and that they are taught vast amounts of information and vividly experience worlds they would otherwise never know. However, they have no chance to use the English, to cope with the information, or to react to the worlds — that is, to think about what they view.

So how should we teachers in our classrooms try to manage television and its effects? Do we condemn it to our students and ban it from the premises and the activities we preside over? Or do we accept it as an inevitable competitor and try to turn it into an ally? I have a few suggestions.

• Condemnation can only be harmful to the education of real television addicts. Television has become so much a part of their personalities and process of thinking and perceiving that to condemn it is, to a considerable extent, to condemn them as people. It's something like rejecting all English that is not standard English. Condemn children's language or their deeply established habits, and they feel themselves condemned, lessened, and antagonized. (This is not to say, let me quickly add, that we do not try to teach all the skills of standard English, which are vital to a person's flourishing in the mainstream of our world.)

• Instead of condemning television, try to use it, to exploit its educational advantages, to show how much better books and talk can be, and to wean students from it. If your students come from families in which books, conversation, and thought are highly valued, the weaning may be easy and the families grateful for your support. If not, not.

• There are occasional programs whose content is so valuable and in which the visual experience is so essential (probing reports on vital community and world situations, debates on contemporary or eternal issues, science demonstrations, travel experiences, real plays genuinely acted) that you and your students, by having experienced them in common, can use them to stimulate classroom discussion and, later, reading and writing. Help in identifying and using good programs is available from the WGBH Educational Foundation, 125 Western Ave., Boston, Mass. 02134; Teachers Guides to Television, 699 Madison Ave., New York, N.Y. 10021; and Prime Time School Television, 120 S. LaSalle St., Chicago, Ill. 60603.

• Show students that a picture on television isn't the whole truth; it's inevitably edited — probably more so than an account in a good newspaper. Have the class compare. I think they will find that television must zip urgently from happening to happening, and vivid though the picture may be, and convincing as it may seem, it is inevitably a mere slice of the whole and therefore a distortion.

• Help students understand the editing (and large amount of cogent writing) that goes into producing a television program by providing them with copies of actual television scripts for study. One source of copies is Capital Cities Television Productions, 4100 City Line Ave., Philadelphia, Pa. 19131. They also provide a television reading program, which, says the Council for Basic Education, "tries to wring educational value out of programs that are popular with kids."

• Don't be afraid to prescribe at least two hours (or however much) of television-off time each evening, when homework must be done and books read. Explain clearly to parents the reason for your prescription and urge them to read, too. The prescription will be stronger if you can get the school's administration of your academic department to give it, rather than you alone.

• A television apparatus that can put programs on cassettes enables the students and you to view together in class certain programs or even commercials that you can then analyze, discuss, and write about. In this way, even the worst stuff can be held up to critical scrutiny (even interrupted and bits repeated), and the best be appreciated and dealt with.

• Cassette taping of a few television examples for use in class can also relieve you of having to watch a lot of television. Now and then, however, to stay in touch with the alternate life, you will have to experience some of it yourself, eye to tube.

14.
Organizing the Time

Hint 106. The teacher should especially guard
against having such a rush of work come to a
focus at the hour of closing that the school
shall be dismissed in confusion.

Abbie G. Hall

In Ingmar Bergman's movie *Scenes from a Marriage,* Marianne
says, "Just think about it. Our life's mapped out into little
squares — every day, every hour, every minute. The squares are
filled, one by one, and in good time. If there's suddenly an
empty square, we're dismayed."
So it is in most schools, even more than in other parts of life.

The master schedule

Almost any class, especially a self-contained one, benefits from
having the basic schedule for the day written on the board or in
some other place where all can see and work from it. This
schedule provides the spine for the day's work.

Once students are out of elementary school, however, and
they study different subjects at different times, the schedule
too often becomes king, security blanket, welcome scapegoat,
excuse for not thinking. Yet we obviously must have schedules
to enable teachers and students to plan ahead and to experience
each day the regularity and routine that a schedule provides.
We all need some of that security, even though we all should,
on occasion, be dismayed and challenged by "suddenly an
empty square."

In 1942, the Eight-Year Study of the Progressive Education
Association reported on its experiment with some thirty
schools that considered themselves and had been chosen as
"progressive." As a part of the experiment, the schools were
liberated, for eight years in the 1930's, from the college-

imposed curriculum requirements against which many of them had been protesting. What happened in some of them was not much, which led the authors of the report to remark, "We have grown to love our chains."

We teachers do indeed grow to love, because we genuinely need them, time blocks within which we can do our work. But the schedule should respond to the educational program, never determine or limit it. We must never be afraid to ask the schedule maker, for whom a neat, nicely working time plan can become a piece of addictive beauty disembodied from its vital purpose, to let up and think flexibly. We should start with the best educational program we can devise, and *then* see if it can be scheduled. But most of us are no good at making schedules. We are much better at seeing all too narrowly and defending passionately our own needs only. In making a schedule — no matter how sophisticated the technique — everyone has to give in order to get a schedule that is best for the whole school.

Ways to manage time within a class period

In Chapter 8, I suggested some ways to make good use of the time called a "period." Here are a few more ways.

• Reserve the first or last ten minutes (or longer) of certain periods as reading and consultation time, when all students know that as part of the routine they are to have some independent, silent work to do, and that they have a chance, if they need it, to talk with you. This is an excellent way to get individual papers dealt with and small problems straightened out. An alternative is to have one entire period a week to be set aside for reading and consultation.

• Schedule, either regularly or when the time and climate are right, brief-feature time (show and tell), when individual students may take a minute or two to tell, explain, act, mime, or show something of special interest, tell a joke, or ask a question. Having a sign-up sheet will let you know whether there is enough to fill the time. Items in brief-feature time need not have anything to do with classwork, though they may add to its scope. You, too, should sign up occasionally.

• Have one day every week or two be presentation day, when some new material — film, skit, lecture, reading aloud, speaker, debate, oral report, a new idea, lesson, or subject matter — is presented and the class mainly listens, takes notes, and asks questions.

• Reserve a writing day, perhaps once every two weeks, when students spend all or part of the period writing and then hand their work in at the end of the period. This exercise gives you a good check on how well students write under pressure of time and without outside help. They may either all write on the same subject or not, as you wish.

• After the school year is under way, or perhaps during the last two or three months of the year, let students develop a plan for independent work or an independent project. (In Chapter 10, where I give specific suggestions for subjects and methods, note especially suggestions for setting guidelines and monitoring progress — or lack of it — of projects.) The class may agree that one or two periods a week will be project days, or that an entire week can be turned over to project work, or that no homework can be given for a certain time because they are doing project work at home instead. Some students will want and be ready for more independent work time than others.

Using time out of school

One way or another, people are being educated or miseducated, in and out of school, all the time, and there's no switch for turning a mind off or on. Here are some thoughts about the time out of school.

Some students and their parents feel that weekends should be kept inviolate, uninvaded by required schoolwork. I've never been able to agree with this view. If what is happening at school has any meaning or momentum, then weekends are going to be important, thick slices of time when students can work independently. We should not, however, be so impressed with our own assignments that we can't appreciate the benefits that many students derive from weekends away from all thoughts of school — pursuing their own interests, taking off with friends, or just plain loafing. We should assign homework far enough ahead to let students plan time for nonschool activities.

The four-day week has become a reality in some places. Most school people do not question the value of three months off in the summer, even though the original reason for it — doing summer work on the farm — no longer exists in most places. But the five-day school week is still almost universal, if only because it coincides with the five-day work week. When schools in Maine switched to a four-day week in order to save fuel, people were surprised to find that the students learned their basic skills as well as or better than they had done during the same number of five-day weeks. A lot of intelligent planning was involved, of course, but the lesson here is that we should not live unexamined lives and that different plans may work better than our usual ones.

Another way to make and use free time

Many schools where students don't have to be under direct, visual supervision all the time allow students to use their free time as they wish, when no class is scheduled.

Some schools let students go wherever they want, even (if parents give blanket written permission) off campus, provided they attend all classes and other scheduled events, such as assemblies and homeroom periods. The grade level at which such freedom can be used beneficially depends on what goes on out of and around the school, but many find that even seventh graders can use such freedom well. More typically, this kind of free time is the privilege of high school juniors and seniors.

The student must understand that this freedom is granted only to those who make good use of it, maintain a satisfactory record, stay out of trouble, meet scheduled obligations. The student must also understand that this privilege may be withdrawn or restricted if the freedom is not used responsibly and in ways that are acceptable to the community.

When it becomes necessary to restrict this freedom, it is usually best to do it for a specific period of time or until a definite goal (such as finishing a paper or achieving a certain level of skill or stopping some kind of behavior) is reached. It is probably a good idea for the student's guidance counselor (or homeroom teacher or grade head) to do the restricting, rather than having just any old teacher "slap the kid into study hall" for the rest of the year, which usually accomplishes absolutely nothing good. Be sure to allow for some consideration and reflection — fairness — before taking drastic action.

More suggestions about time

The following suggestions can prove as successful as they are simple — for they work.

• Have a large clock in each room, from nursery school on up. If you are the only one wearing a watch, and only a bell marks the ends of periods, students miss out on a constant low-key opportunity to adjust to the real demands of time. Clocks do not strengthen the tyranny of time; rather, they oblige time to show its face so that it can be dealt with as a reality, out in the open, instead of being hidden until, at the bell, it jumps out at student and teacher alike. Good teachers in a conventional school are always aware of what time it is — time of day, and how far into the period they are — and adjust their plans accordingly. Students, too should be aware of the time.

• Post your schedule and an appointment sign-up sheet. Put your schedule in a conspicuous place so that everyone can see at a glance when you are and are not available, with free periods clearly marked. You can have the sign-up sheet in the room or outside the door, in case you're teaching, for students who need to see you to sign up for free time during or after school.

• Grant groups of teachers a large block or two of time each day. Small groups of teachers who are primarily responsible for teaching all the students in one "house" can use this time for scheduling their own time and that of their students as well as use of available space. Often the staff of a small "school within a school" can work out a schedule that is more flexible than the one for the entire school. Because it takes skill and experience to design a schedule like this, it is a good idea to consult an expert schedule maker on the staff, who can often see booby traps, point out places where even more flexibility can be built into the schedule, and help the mini-school's plan to mesh well with that of the whole school.

• If possible, schedule a period for teachers' meetings. In this way, teachers don't have to count on making random arrangements. If a meeting isn't needed on a given day, everyone will greatly appreciate this unexpected gift of free time.

15.
Evaluating and Testing
the Performance of Students

Hint 14. Establish a system of bookkeeping. Each pupil keeping his own account of debit and credit. A failure or misdemeanor being entered on the debit side and each perfect day in deportment on the credit side. At the end of the week they must balance their books and report.   *Abbie G. Hall*

Note carefully, in this chapter, that we are talking about evaluating the performance of students, not the students themselves.

A few years ago, a *New Yorker* cartoon by Whitney Darrow showed a nasty-looking little kid and his puzzled mother in the office of the school counselor, who is saying confidently, "Mrs. Minton, there's no such thing as a bad boy. Hostile, perhaps. Aggressive, recalcitrant, even sadistic. But not *bad.*"

This is the truth, and we mustn't forget it: we find bad performance, bad behavior, but not bad boys or girls. Whenever we are called upon to evaluate, our job is to describe, as objectively as possible, the academic performance and school behavior of our students. We are not there to evaluate our students as people.

What should teachers evaluate?

Certainly, we are on soundest ground if we stick to testing and evaluating the academic skills and knowledge of our students. However, as we consider their work and progress, we should not separate schoolwork from other behavior, because "nonacademic" behavior often helps to explain academic performance, good and bad.

We need to keep our eyes and ears open, because how our students feel and behave affects how well they can learn. We should note at the end of each day those who are having diffi-

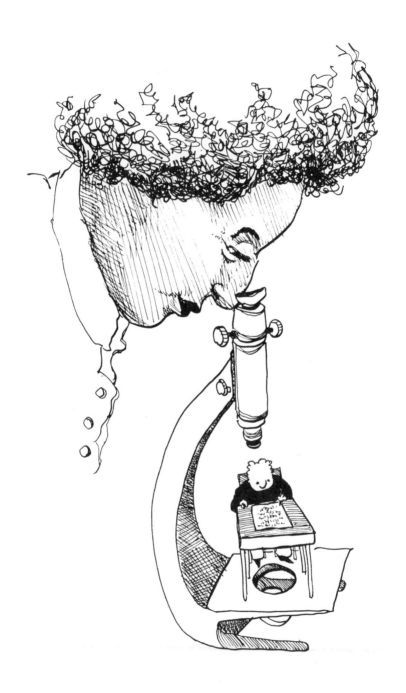

culty or causing trouble. We should know who seems troubled, who acts nervous, who sulks, who never talks, who is "hostile, aggressive, recalcitrant, even sadistic," and when and how (but not why; that is not up to us to judge). We should also know who seems friendly, healthily competitive, cooperative, and even altruistic.

Many schools have as one of their main purposes, or their primary purpose, to help their students develop sound values, whether American values, democratic values, religious values, humanistic values, or a combination of these. While I am convinced that values are the most important thing you can learn in school, I am also certain that we are never justified in marking or grading students on their values. But we can and probably should try to be ready with an opinion, a comment, or even a grade, on what the typical report card calls "citizenship" — assuming responsibility, cooperating, developing and obeying rules, respecting property, working and playing well with others, being courteous — and "work habits" — making good use of time and materials, doing neat and careful work, completing assignments on time, putting forth good effort.

Now let's turn to the primary job of evaluation: testing and measuring academic skills and knowledge of subject matter.

Why do we test?

We test to get data that we can use. It's a waste of time to give more tests than we can use, and there's no point in spending time and money for a lot of tests and then filing the results, for later use just in case.

We test to obtain information for ourselves and other teachers, for students, for parents, for the school, and for the community that supports the school. Test data can be used (1) to inform students how well they are doing, where their strengths and weaknesses lie, and what they should do about them; (2) to inform parents about the academic progress of their children; (3) to give you and the rest of the faculty information to use in planning for and with each student and each class; (4) to tell the school how well it is doing in developing skills and teaching subject matter and how, if need be, it should change its program; (5) to help everyone involved decide where a student should be placed in school; (6) to give schools, colleges, and professional schools some idea whether students are likely to do well if admitted; and (7) to tell the community how well its school or schools are doing.

Some terms and concepts of testing

I have always been surprised by how little many teachers actually know about testing and about the kinds of things different tests do and do not measure. Here are some basic terms and concepts that all teachers should know if they are to make and use tests intelligently.

Valid and invalid tests. If a test has high validity, it tests what it is supposed to test. This is not as funny as it sounds, for it is probably the most important thing to know about a test. For example, a test consisting of ten simple subtraction problems, with no time limit, is a valid test of the ability to subtract. But a test consisting of twenty-five such problems, each involving two long numbers and to be finished in three minutes, is a test not only of ability to subtract but also of speed and keeping cool under pressure, so this test is less valid. Sometimes tests are invalid for reasons of which we may be totally unaware. Here are three examples.

A son of mine always scored in the high 90's in a college economics course for which he didn't do much of the reading because he was able to tell which answers on long multiple-choice tests *sounded* right. So he was an expert in reading the professor's mind, not in economics.

A language study showed that children in a Pittsburgh ghetto, as part of their daily speech, used some 3,800 words, expressions, and constructions that did not appear in dictionaries and grammars of standard English. Tests of standard English were therefore invalid measures of the language ability of these children because the children did not habitually use most of the vocabulary of the tests.

According to one study, the Scholastic Aptitude Test of the College Board is a valid predictor of a student's ability to succeed (that is, to get good grades in college) but an invalid test of likely later success and satisfaction in the professions — medicine, architecture, education, law. According to other studies, a valid predictor of success and satisfaction in life after college is a complete and accurate list of achievement in extracurricular activities in school and college.

So when we give tests, we must figure as best we can whether the tests we are giving are doing what we want them to — whether they are valid.

Reliable and unreliable tests. A reliable test is one that gives about the same results every time. A five-item true-false test is not a reliable test of the content of a unit, course, or book because the sampling of information is too small. Different students whose real knowledge of the subject matter might be equal can easily get quite different scores on such a sketchy test. Other unreliable results are produced by giving tests just before lunch, or just after a fight, or by giving tests in which the questions are quickly read aloud once or written illegibly on the board. To be reliable, a test must be given under uniform conditions each time and contain a broad sampling of the content or skills being tested.

Objective and subjective tests. Many teachers feel that if a test has lots of items, and if each item has a correct answer, and if the whole thing adds up to a definite score, it is an objective test. Well, it is, to the extent that the score is not affected by the test scorer's attitude toward the person being tested, the handwriting on the test, or how the person marking the test is feeling that day. The test may not be objective in the usual sense of the word, however, if test items tend to favor a particular type of student, or if things other than knowledge and skills — like students' attitudes toward the teacher — affect the results. A single, well-constructed essay question or a series of carefully composed brief-answer questions may actually, if read and graded skillfully, be more objective than a long series of test items that produce a score.

Aptitude test. This test supposedly measures aptitude for certain academic or other work, not actual achievement in the field. A well-known aptitude test is the College Board's Scholastic Aptitude Test (SAT), which is widely used to measure aptitude for college work. The SAT is scored on a scale of 200-800, with 500 the median (middle) score, based on comparison with others bound for college. The SAT yields a verbal score, a mathematical score, and a total score. A person who scores 675 on the verbal section, 730 on math, a total of 1,405, has high aptitude for college work. One who scores V 325, M 310, total 635, has low aptitude. However, such is life, and such are tests, that some 650-score people do well in college, and some 1,400-score ones do not. Another widely used group of aptitude tests comes from the American College Testing Service (ACT). The ACT tests are actually a combination of aptitude and achievement measures. Scores on ACT tests generally range from 10 to 36, with 28-30 being roughly equivalent to a 600 on the SAT. Every year, more and more colleges are using ACT tests as a measure of applicants' ability for admission.

Intelligence test. An intelligence test is a special kind of aptitude test that measures "intelligence," whatever that is. Whether or not intelligence can be measured is an unsettled question. We all know bright people who act stupid and dull people who have common sense and good judgment. But there are mental tasks that some people perform better than others, such as recall and memory, reasoning, defining, using numbers, solving problems — the kinds of things that one is likely to be asked to do in school.

An intelligence test determines a person's mental age, that is, whether he is able to do mental tasks at the level of a typical person of a given age — up to age sixteen, when those parts of intelligence measured by intelligence tests are considered to have reached their peak and not to increase with age. Child A, ten years old, has a mental age scored at 14, and thus has a higher intelligence score than Child B, also ten, but whose mental age is nine. The score is given as an intelligence quotient, or IQ, the result of dividing the mental age by the chronological age:

$$\text{Child A} \quad \text{MA 14/CA 10} = \text{IQ 140}$$
$$\text{Child B} \quad \text{MA 9/CA 10} = \text{IQ 90}$$

Theoretically, the average intelligence score is 100, meaning that the average person's mental and chronological ages are the same.

Everyone acknowledges that many difficult, perhaps impossible, problems are connected with measuring intelligence. Test makers try to use subjects to which everyone tested has had the same exposure, but this is obviously impossible, so every IQ test is to some degree a measure of experience, not "intelligence."

There are all kinds of reasons why people do poorly on IQ tests, even though they are not stupid. Perhaps the test is in English, and the child taking it speaks mostly Spanish, or the child is sick, afraid, nervous, or missed breakfast, or is worried about something that is going on at home. Any child working under these conditions will do worse on the test than a child who feels good about everything. For these reasons, I think it is very important for us, when we speak of intelligence tests, to say "IQ score," not just "IQ," in order to avoid making an absolute statement about intelligence.

This is far from saying that an IQ test is of no value, however. A child with a high IQ score should do well in school, even though one with a low IQ score may also do well. But if the students tested have relatively typical backgrounds and experience, then their IQ scores do provide important information for use in planning their education.

One other point about IQ tests. Most schools give fairly short tests, administered to a group, that rely on the ability to read and, in some cases, to listen. These group tests, inexpensive and easy to score, are much less valid and reliable than individually administered tests. A much better, but more expensive, example of an individually administered test is the Wechsler Intelligence Scale for Children (WISC). This test doesn't rely much on reading ability and provides several subscores that allow the experienced test giver to give the school a helpful analysis of a child's mental ability. If a school can afford it, I think all children in third or fourth grade should be given the WISC, whose results can be used to measure the rest of their school performance. If that is too expensive, then at least all the children who seem to be having academic problems should be given the WISC as an early step in diagnosis. Maybe they have genuinely low intelligence and should not be asked to do hard work in school. But if they have been doing poorly and score high on the WISC, or parts of it, further study and diagnosis are called for.

Parents tend to rely too much on IQ scores and to see them as tremendously significant, almost magic numbers that can be used to compare their own children with one another and with other people's children. Other parents, equally wrong, believe that IQ scores don't mean a thing. For these reasons, I think it's best not to give out IQ scores or, if we do, only after very careful interpretation.

Achievement test. This test differs from an aptitude or an intelligence test in that it measures information acquired and skills developed in specific subjects taught in schools, not general knowledge. Achievement tests are useful for discovering whether students have learned what their teachers set out to teach them. The best of these tests are made up after careful study of what students in American schools are supposed to know, and they are revised from time to time to keep them up with changes in curriculum. The College Board Achievement Tests are widely used as a measure of knowledge of subject matter in connection with admission to college, as are the ACT tests. Another widely used test is the Stanford Achievement Test, one of several commercial tests that measure the progress of students through school.

Standardized test. A standardized test is one that has been tried out on a large number of students to establish a standard of performance, or norm, for various grades or ages on the various sections of the test. Most tests published by large companies are standardized to enable you to compare the performance of your students with that of the "average" student of the same age and, to some extent, background. By contrast, a teacher-made test is not standardized, except against a standard that the teacher has established mentally or on the basis of experience with the test over several years.

Criterion-referenced test. In this kind of test, students' scores are compared with a fixed standard of achievement, not with the performance of other students. For example, a school might decide that the criterion for promotion to the next grade is 80 per cent right answers on a reading comprehension test, a factual biology test, a factual history test, a math test, or whatever. If all students reach 80 per cent, all are promoted. If only half do, only half are promoted, and the other half are given additional instruction until they reach 80 per cent.

Raw score. In any test, the number of items the student gets right is the raw score. It has little meaning until it is compared with raw scores of other students. This comparison is commonly expressed as a percentile or as a grade equivalent.

Norm. A norm is simply a standard against which to compare the performance of an individual or class. Norms are published for most widely used tests. The norms for such tests are usually based on the performance of public school pupils across the nation. For schools that are highly selective, these norms are often not very helpful because so many of their students cluster near the top of the scale. For this reason, "independent school norms" have been established for some tests, comparing the scores of pupils with those of other pupils in similarly selective schools, thus making it possible to discriminate more finely among the performance scores of academically able students. These special norms are useful for public and private schools where most of the students expect to attend highly selective colleges.

Percentile. When a test is being standardized or "normed," all the scores of the sample group who took the test are arranged from lowest to highest and then divided into 100 groups of equal size, with each 100th being a percentile. The bottom group is in the 0th percentile, the top in the 99th, and the middle, or median (not average, or mean) group is in the 50th percentile. Percentile does not mean the per cent correct; it denotes where, on a scale of 0-99, a student's score places him in relation to the scores of other students whose scores were used in standardizing the test.

Grade equivalent. The other way of giving meaning to the raw scores of tests compares them with the scores that a typical student at a certain grade level in an average public school gets, according to the best statistical analysis that can be done. Thus, if a student gets grade-equivalent scores of 6.4 in vocabulary, 8.3 in reading comprehension, 5.2 in arithmetic reasoning, and 4.8 in arithmetic computation, it means that on *this* test, at the time it was given, he has performed on the vocabulary section of the test like an average student in the fourth month of sixth grade, and so on through the other sections.

Statistical significance. Small differences among the scores of students are not likely to mean much, to be statistically significant. For example, a student scoring in the 57th percentile on reading comprehension cannot with any certainty be said to be a much better reader than one scoring in the 55th percentile, nor can one with a grade equivalent of 10.6 be said to be better than one scoring 10.3. There are just too many chance factors entering into a test situation and too many ingredients in what we call "reading comprehension" to justify such fine distinctions. All reputable published standardized tests tell how much difference in scores there must be for that difference to be considered significant. Be sure to read the manuals that come with these tests so that you will understand how much to rely on scores and differences among them.

Practice effect. Other things being equal, people who have had lots of practice taking tests are likely to do better on them than people who haven't. Good published tests always give a couple of items for practice before starting the items that count, plus plain directions to be read aloud so that everyone will have a chance to practice and thus minimize the differences caused by the practice effect. As mentioned earlier, some students have temporary problems that interfere with their test taking. Others have real difficulties with various mechanics of taking tests (circling answers, keeping track of the right place on a separate answer sheet, etc.), difficulties that have absolutely no connection with the subject matter or skill being tested. So, with students who get low scores on tests but who are doing perfectly well in the schoolwork that is being tested, you should be skeptical about these low scores and perhaps ask the students if the mechanics of the test caused them any trouble. Chapter 18 gives some hints on helping students take tests.

Prejudice effect. It is a sad fact that some teachers give better marks to students who score well on standardized tests than to those who perform equally well in school but whose test scores are low. *Pygmalion in the Classroom*, by Robert Rosenthal and Lenore Jacobson (New York: Holt, Rinehart & Winston, 1968), tells of a test Harvard University administered to a group of children that was supposed to show which ones were about to experience a learning spurt and which ones weren't. Test scores were given to the children's teachers, who were told that the testers wanted to find out whether their test was valid by comparing the scores with actual classroom performance. Lo and behold, the children whose learning was supposed to spurt were those who got much better marks than the others, and the test seemed to be valid. However, the learning-spurt scores had, in fact, been faked, and the whole thing was a ruse in order to measure the effects of teacher expectation (positive prejudice, in this case) on pupil performance. The testers concluded that if a teacher *thinks* pupils are bright and will do well, they are much more likely to do so, even if the only measured difference between the do-well's and the so-so's is the teacher's opinion.

It is important for teachers to use test scores as items of information to help them plan intelligently with students for their assignments, reading, course choices, and other work. It is equally important for teachers to evaluate students' actual work without reference to standardized test scores, unless the objective of a course is to do well on a standardized achievement test in the subject taught.

Correlation and causation. A great many people assume, mistakenly, that because two things go together one of them is the cause of the other. It has been found, for example, that students who take Latin tend to get better scores on word tests than people who don't take Latin. This does not, however, prove that Latin causes people to get better scores. It might simply mean that the more verbal people go into Latin and therefore, naturally, do better on verbal tests. We should be very careful to keep in mind the fact that correlation and cause are two different things, that umbrellas do not cause rain.

16.
Using and Misusing Published Tests

Hint 114. If a record has been kept by your predecessor, study it carefully.

Abbie G. Hall

From time to time in the educational cycle, it is fashionable to debunk commercially published tests as unjust, inaccurate, and perniciously judgmental. A recent cartoon shows a group of educators solemnly reporting, "It is the opinion of this committee that literacy tests are heavily weighted in favor of those who can read and write."

There is no question that standardized tests can be used by schools and teachers in ways that are harmful to students. Tests may use one kind of language, the student another; some bright children are poor test takers; some test items seem to penalize the extra bright, who see things in them that the item writers did not see, and so they pick the "wrong" answers. Students get low scores firmly stuck on them, so they think they're dumb, their parents think they're dumb, their teachers teach them as if they were dumb, they get an unshakable record of being dumb, and they naturally develop feelings of inferiority and discouragement. The result is, to use Jonathan Kozol's phrase, "death at an early age."

Ways to avoid the bad effects of tests

Tests do not need to be used in these ways, however. Here are some suggestions for avoiding these educational disasters.

• Never use a test score or set of test scores as the sole criterion for judging the performance of students or estimating their potential performance. Test scores should be considered as important bits of information to be used in conjunction with a lot of other information.

• If a student gets low test scores but performs well in his schoolwork, judge him by his work, not by his scores.

• As a rule, don't tell students what their standardized test scores are, and don't tell their parents, either. If, for some reason, you think it would be helpful to tell them, explain carefully the limited importance and the many possiblities for error of such scores.

• Use test scores mainly to help plan students' work and the materials you use to teach your classes.

• If there is a large gap between a student's scores and other performance, try to find out why.

• If some students seem to be poor test takers but otherwise intelligent, try to teach them to learn to be better test takers. (See Chapter 18 for suggestions.)

• If a student makes a very low score on a group intelligence test, try to get the school to give him an individually administered test, like the Wechsler Intelligence Scale for Children (see page 125) before deciding that his academic intelligence is low.

• Never tell students or their parents their IQ scores unless you are certain it will have a helpful effect. The label "IQ" has too much magic attached to it to be received realistically.

• Don't forget that on any standardized test, if it is properly standardized (if the norms are correct), half of all the students who take it are inevitably going to score at the middle or below, and half at the middle or above. In your school, you may have more students in the bottom or the top half, but this is no basis for judging the teaching excellence of the school. (See more on this in Chapter 20.) After all, on any proper test half of all the students in all schools will score at grade level or below, and half at grade level or above.

• If you teach in a school that admits only bright, college-bound students, and you use special "independent school norms," remember that testing below the 50th percentile does not mean "below average" in comparison to the population as a whole.

• If in doubt, and if you must, use test scores to encourage students, but never to shame or discourage.

• Don't beat a student over the head with a high IQ score. For legitimate reasons entirely beyond his control, he may not be able to work up to what his IQ score leads you to believe should be his standard. Instead, try to find out why he isn't working as well as his IQ score leads you to believe he should.

• I repeat: in general, use test scores only for planning work and assignments, and consider them only as one piece of possibly important information. And *never* compare the test scores of students in public.

A typical standardized test

Over the years, I have examined the administrative procedures and content of many widely used standardized achievement tests. I have also worked as a "subject matter expert" in constructing multiple-choice items for one of the most reputable, careful, and conscientious test publishers. I believe that the major published tests are useful instruments, but that they have limited purposes and should be held firmly within their complicated educational context.

Before describing a typical test, I should explain how the content is selected. A careful survey is made of the curriculum and materials of large numbers of schools across the country, and items are based on the content that is most commonly found in them. Obviously, to the extent that teachers teach for the tests, this process has a tendency to push education toward a central core. Even so, the core is probably a better place to tend toward than the fringes. If a school believes itself to be on a fringe (and there are lots of excellent fringes), it should make allowances for this as it considers testing and test results.

How are multiple-choice items constructed? To read the criticisms of them, you might think that they are constructed ploddingly, capriciously, or carelessly, but the facts are otherwise. From the selected body of content, teams of item writers make up items and then try them out on two or three other item writers to catch those that don't work — they can't agree on what the correct answer is, or they find that certain words or language in an item are misleading.

Then the items are put together in a test and tried out in several classrooms to see which ones work. When an "item analysis" of the test is made, it turns out that some items everyone gets right (of no use for a test) and some items everyone gets wrong (also of no use). With some other items, the people who do well on the entire test are more likely to get wrong answers than people who do poorly; these items have a surprise reverse twist and are discarded.

After this long process is completed, a test made up of items that are shown by actual experience to work well with most groups most of the time can be constructed. So the whole business is far from haphazard.

Typical of the good tests is the Stanford Achievement Test. One form of its Advanced Battery, designed, roughly, for grades 7-9, consists of items dealing with vocabulary, reading comprehension, mathematics concepts, computation, and applications, spelling, language, social science, and science. Each section of the test, which contains anywhere from 12 to 79 items, is allotted 20, 30, or 35 minutes, for a total of 260 minutes, or four hours and 20 minutes.

If you look at the Stanford Achievement Test as a whole and with an unbiased eye, I think you are likely to conclude that it and tests like it are carefully constructed and that they do a pretty good job of measuring a student's knowledge and achievement in the areas they claim to test (assuming that the students have been living in more or less "typical" homes and have been through a more or less typical American school curriculum — assumptions that obviously cannot be made for every student and apply hardly at all to students whose backgrounds differ from those of most Americans or those who go to schools that offer a curriculum that differs markedly from the usual middle-of-the-road curriculum).

An all-school testing program

If I were in charge of a typical school or were a teacher who had some influence on my school's educational program, I would advocate that each year the school give all students, starting about third grade, the sections of a good standardized test series that measure vocabulary, reading comprehension, mathematical reasoning, concepts, and applications, and "language." Such testing provides a good standardized measure of the skills that are applicable to any academic situation (and to many life situations). This kind of testing tends to counteract wishful thinking — about how this student or that one will improve with age and without any special attention from us — and to keep us honest. It is far less important to have a standardized measure of subject-matter content, which varies and should vary from school to school and from class to class.

For students who are bound for college, a school should switch in the top two grades to the tests especially designed to measure what the colleges expect — either the College Board's Scholastic Aptitude and Achievement tests or the American College Testing Program (ACT) — and should be sure that students take the preliminary forms (if any) as well as the final forms of the tests.

17.
Making and
Grading Your Own Tests

Hint 62. There are two ways in which teachers injure and use ill-memory. They give it no variety of work or they refuse all exercise whatever.   *Abbie G. Hall*

Probably most school testing consists of teacher-made quizzes, true-false tests, multiple-choice tests, and exams. The main advantage of good teacher-made tests is that they test what has been taught. The main disadvantage, especially for teachers of limited experience, is that such tests give few clues to how well students are doing compared to how well they should be doing, in relation both to their own abilities and to what is normally expected of students of the same age and grade. Teacher-made tests can also be far too "tough" and discouraging, especially if a teacher relishes a reputation as being a "hard" teacher.

On the other hand, a teacher who is anxious to please, too concerned about the supposed fragility and sensitivity of students, and not willing to risk overchallenging pupils may give tests that are far too easy and unrealistically encouraging, which can lead to wishful thinking and unrealistic planning on the part of students who are given artificially high grades.

In general, I have found that most teachers spend too little time making up their tests and then too much time mopping up after them.

Types of teacher-made tests

Multiple-choice tests. Although it takes a lot of time and care to make up a workable multiple-choice test, a good one can save you hours in evaluating how well students have mastered a broad area of subject matter and how soundly they are able to think about it. If you are likely to be teaching the same body of subject matter (a book, a period of history, a science unit) to several sections or for more than one year and plan to use the same teaching materials, it is worth taking the time to devise a multiple-choice test that covers it. Here are some suggestions on how to go about it.

• Be sure that the reading level of the test items is not beyond any of your students.

• When you've made a first draft, try it out on someone who knows the subject to see whether any items are misleading in some unsuspected way and then revise those that are.

• Be careful that the "wrong" answers *sound* as correct as the right answer. Some words, like "never" and "always," tip savvy test takers off to a "wrong" answer.

• Be careful not to make your "right" answers consistently longer and more carefully qualified than your "wrong" ones.

• Here and there, throw in an answer that is so clearly "wrong" that it is funny. This can do wonders for class morale.

• Avoid trick questions.

• A duplicated test is far better than one read aloud. Reading aloud is ponderous, does not allow for different rates of pondering, is not much use as practice for test taking in general, and lets the observant ignoramus see when most people are checking a certain question and check that one too. Similarly, a duplicated answer sheet makes life easier for all concerned.

• One trouble with most multiple-choice tests is that they have three "wrong" answers and one right one, thus bombarding students with lots of incorrect information, some of which they may "learn," consciously or unconsciously, while taking the test. Instead, try using this form: "All but *one* of the following statements are true. Which one is false?"

• To be sure that students understand how to do the test and use the answer sheet, give them a couple of practice items that do not count — especially important with the "which one is false" type of item.

• After correcting the tests, analyze the answers and discuss with the class any questions that most people got wrong. This is a very good way to help students get unconfused and master the subject.

• Since some students finish multiple-choice tests far more

quickly than others, try giving an extra-credit written-answer question or two at the end, to avoid the fidgets and the dribbling departures that demoralize and distract those who haven't finished.

True-false tests. These are not much use because it is hard to find items that require more than superficial understanding and yet are not misleading. Especially bad are short true-false tests (15-20 items) that count heavily in judging a student's work. But short true-false tests do make a good introduction to discussion of a subject after students have puzzled over each item. Tests used thus should not be marked, just scored.

Short-answer tests. A useful, simple test is one that asks a good question or two and allows students 10 to 15 minutes to write. Make sure that your questions are clear and that they cannot be answered just "Yes" or "No" or in a single sentence. Ending your questions with "Why?" or "Explain" is usually a good idea.

Examinations. These longer tests cover the work of a semester or an entire year. It is sensible for you to consider, and to let your students know that you do, that an examination is not mainly a hurdle to be got over or a hardship to be endured but rather an opportunity for students to show how much they know and how clearly they can think, organize, and write. Preparing for and taking an exam (see Chapter 18) can and should be part of learning, not just a storage and regurgitation exercise. Here are some suggestions for making, giving, and marking exams.

● Two- and three-hour exams do not work well for most students in junior high school and below, who do better started off with short exams or parts of exams.

● A typical exam is made up of several questions or sections of several types: multiple-choice, short-answer, and a longer essay question or two. You can allow students some choice— "Answer any three of the following five questions," for example.

● Make clear how much time to spend on (and thus how much weight is attached to) each question so that students won't get carried away by less important questions and use their time unwisely.

● Make it clear whether students are required to stay for the entire time and, if they are, either tell people to bring something to read or give extra-credit questions at the end of the exam.

• When marking exams, try to be objective. Think of what is on the paper, not of who wrote it. Since it is easy after reading a very good or very poor answer to one question to be influenced in judging answers to the next question, I suggest reading and marking the answers to question 1 on all the papers, then doing the same for question 2, and so on.

• Give a separate mark or other indication for whatever spelling and punctuation errors do not affect your ability to understand what the writer means. I think it is nonsense to "count off" for spelling when an exam is testing some other subject entirely. Even so, students are probably helped by knowing that you have noticed the mechanics of their papers. If you don't they get the idea that you only have to spell or punctuate correctly in English.

• Because exams are a wonderful way for students to find out what they have done wrong and how they might do better, urge your school to schedule exams in a way that will allow you ample time to discuss them afterwards in class and with students who wish to talk to you individually.

Establishing grades for teacher-made tests

A problem with teacher-made tests is how to mark them fairly. Do you simply say that getting 60 per cent or more of the items correct is passing, 70 per cent fair, 80 per cent good, and 90 per cent excellent? When there is a variety of types of items and questions, do you establish a value for each item and question, so that the whole thing adds up to 100, and then figure students' scores and grades accordingly?

In Chapter 21, I discuss quite thoroughly the advantages and disadvantages of giving grades and having a marking system. Here, let me simply say that, if marks are used, you and your students should consider them as specific pieces of information of limited usefulness, not as coin to be earned or general evaluations of personal worth.

School people have a fixation on the scale of 100, of which the section 60-100 is most used, to evaluate student performance. For the purposes of marking tests, let's assume that we'll use, instead, the marks A (excellent), B (good), C (fair), D (poor), and NC (no credit). If you want, or if your school requires you, to convert these letters into numbers, you can figure that A = 90-100, B = 80-89, C = 70-79, D = 60-69, and NC = anything below 60.

Assume you're giving for the first time a 60-item multiple-choice test that you have constructed to cover the factual material in a unit of social studies. Here are the steps I suggest you go through to establish the grades you will give.

1. *Correct the tests and write down each person's raw score.* If there are four options for each test item, the raw score is calculated by taking the number correct and subtracting *one third* of the number wrong. (Subtracting this one third removes the effect of random guessing, since, on the average, if a student marked the items at random he would by chance get one in four, or 15 out of 60, correct, and three out of four, or 45 out of 60, wrong; 15 minus one third of 45 is zero, which is what his score should be if he knows nothing. If there are five options on each item, you subtract *one quarter* the number wrong. This subtraction removes the advantage that a person would have who spent the last moments of the test rapidly and randomly marking all the items he had not finished. He would, by the laws of chance, neither benefit from nor be penalized by doing this. The subtraction does not penalize guessing — in fact, intelligent guessing works to the student's advantage. It only removes the advantage of random guessing.

2. *Write down the distribution of all the students' raw scores.* Say a total of 51 students in two sections have taken the test. The distribution might look like this, with three people scoring 59, two scoring 57, four scoring 54, and so on. (Most people list them in a single long column; they are shown in several smaller columns here.)

59	52	50	43	40	30
59	51	49	43	38	30
59	51	45	43	38	30
57	51	45	42	38	22
57	51	45	40	35	22
54	51	45	40	35	17
54	51	45	40	35	
54	50	44	40	35	
54	50	43	40	31	

3. *Find the median (middle) score.* You do this by counting to the middle, down from the top and up from the bottom. In this case, where there is a total of 51 scores, the score of 44 — which is in the 26th, or middle, position — is the median. (If there had been an even number of scores, say, 50, you would count down from the top and up from the bottom to get the *two* middle scores and divide their sum by 2; if the two middle numbers were 45 and 44, your median would be 44½.)

4. *Decide what mark to assign to the median score.* In order to make this decision, you have to think about such things as your class, the subject matter, your teaching, and how hard the students have worked. If you teach in a school where the students are quite able and work quite well, you should probably decide that B (good) would be a fair mark for an average student in the class (even though the median score, 44, is only just over 74 per cent right).

5. *Now, distribute the marks.* Here's what might be a reasonable distribution: A = scores of 59-57; A− = 54-52; B+ = 51-50; B = 45-44; B− = 44-43; C+ = 40; C = 38; C− = 35; D = 31-30; NC = 22-17. Referring to the columns of scores above, note that there are 10 A's, 20 B's, and a total of only seven D's and NC's. Does that mean you're "inflating" grades? Not at all. It means that most people did well, which is how it should be in the school and situation that I have described.

Some comments on test results

When, say, two thirds of a class does poorly on a test or exam, it is possible that they have been goofing off or that the materials and methods used for teaching have been poor. In either case, everyone who cares, whether teacher or student, should be shaken a bit. Such a shaking can be healthy, provided it results in better work and better teaching that lead to mastery of the material by almost everyone. Unless a group knows very well that it simply hasn't done the work, it is bad practice to leave a class with a substantial proportion of no-credit or fail marks among its members. Some reteaching and retesting are probably called for.

There are too many ways to mark tests and exams to discuss them in detail here. Instead, just let me make four additional points.

- Take *great* care in devising a system for marking tests and exams.
- Explain the system to your classes so that it will be clear and fair.
- Never forget that your marking is subjective because you are comparing the performance of students with what you think it should be, based on your knowledge of the subject and the skills needed to deal with it on a test.
- Don't treat your marks with undue reverence, and be sure your students don't. Marks are just fallible evaluations of a given set of performances at a given time. There is no divine truth in them.

A few more points picked up on testing and evaluation

Before leaving this subject, I think it is important to make a few more points about what tests are and are not for, how they do and do not work.

- If a test is really good and covers most of the territory dealt with in the course, unit, book, or whatever else is being tested, there is no reason why students shouldn't have it in advance and use it to give direction to their study and review. After all, one of the main purposes of a course is for students to learn the material. If having the test in advance will help them do that, why not?
- A similar comment can be made about open-book tests. Unless memorized facts are being tested, using books to answer exam questions can only provide another opportunity to learn. Students should be told, however, that spending most of the test time thumbing through books will not leave them time to write good answers.
- A good way to stimulate students to think about what they are learning is to ask them to submit questions for the test or exam in whatever form they prefer, ranging from multiple-choice to essay questions.
- If you are testing skills, especially reading and dealing with figures, and even spelling and proper use of conventional English, test early enough in the year to leave time to deal with

any weaknesses that are discovered. Also, if you discover (by tests or any other means) a remediable academic weakness that has not been dealt with by the end of the school year, or that still needs more work, be sure to pass the word on to next year's teacher so that special work can be started early.

• If a student gets low scores in reading or math, and you have reason to believe that he or she is intelligent enough to do better, talk to the school's guidance or testing specialists to see about diagnostic testing, which might give more precise evidence on the nature of the problem.

• It is especially important not to ignore weakness in reading, that absolutely essential skill. If a student is reading well below his grade level, the school's first concern should be to try to find out why and then to deal with the problem. Because most reading problems are complicated, superficial remedial instruction is usually not enough; scores increase briefly but fall back soon after the special instruction stops. Careful individual or small-group teaching, based on an expert diagnosis of the problem, is necessary. Also, a school should never be satisfied, or try to calm concerned parents, by saying, "Stop worrying; the child will outgrow the problem."

• The results of standardized tests should be kept in a form that makes them easily available to teachers, one that does not require a lot of digging through the files. As an English teacher, I find it useful to note in my record book the reading and other language-related scores of each student I teach, any IQ scores that are available, and possibly even math scores, too, for purposes of comparison. This easily seen information guides me as I talk with students about their reading and help plan their instruction. I firmly believe that if teachers maintain a professional attitude toward students and their test scores they can use test information helpfully, remembering also that test scores can give too low or too high an estimate of a student's ability. At the very least, scores tell who is very able and should probably be doing better.

• Some measurement-minded people go hog wild on tests, try to measure everything, and have little time for things that can't be measured. Most teachers will be sensible if they are satisfied to use measures of what is obviously measurable and to continue teaching also for the development of the immeasurables. Probably the most important parts of learning — style, expression, appreciation, development of values — cannot be measured by any standardized test.

• One of the most harmful uses of tests is to rank students in order of ability or in order of scores. Such a practice simply discourages those who need encouragement and encourages those who need it least. A rank listing contains no useful information. Ranking tends to set student competing against student in a way that is totally extraneous to the matter being learned. If rank in class figures are required by colleges as part of admission, they should probably be given but kept confidential and never revealed to students or their parents.

• Careful observers of young children report that even those who enter the worst schools from the least promising backgrounds enter school expecting to succeed. The idea that they will fail, all too easily converted into the much worse idea that they *are* failures, is something they learn at school. Tests or marks should never be used to teach this terrible idea.

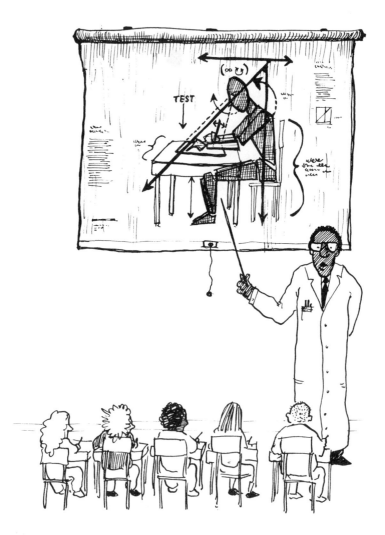

18.
Should You Teach
Students How To Take Tests?

Hint 95. Have the school room well
ventilated. . . . Impure air enervates both leader
and children and sows the seeds of disease.

Abbie G. Hall

Teaching students to do as well as they can on tests is quite different from teaching *for* a test. Teaching *how* to take tests can be a legitimate and useful exercise. One of the very best teachers is simply experience in taking tests.

Preparing for standardized tests

Even though good standardized tests give clear enough directions and a few carefully devised practice items, many students do experience troubles that have little to do with their knowledge of the subject matter or with the skills supposedly being tested and thus may need help.

I say "may" need help; it is only honest to point out that in teaching your students how to take these tests you are giving them a certain advantage over the students whose performances were originally used in establishing the standards for the tests. Thus you may be inflating the scores (and grade equivalents and percentiles) of your students and making their performance look better than it really is as well as your own teaching and the teaching in your school. Do you want to do that?

Here, for better or worse, are ways you can help your students do well on tests.

● Give them facsimile answer sheets on which they can practice marking their answers, just to see how the system works.

● Read the directions for the test to the students a day or so in advance so that they'll be familiar with them.

• Duplicate some very easy questions in exactly the same form as those on the actual test and let students practice on these, just to get the idea. This exercise will also help them to manage the test booklet, the answer sheet, the pencil, and the operations that require good hand-eye coordination.

• If students are not penalized for guessing on a particular test (if the score is simply the number correct), tell them to spend the last moments quickly filling in all the items they have not yet completed.

• Tell students to work as fast as they can without being utterly careless, and never to puzzle a long time over an item but to come back to it if there is time.

• Give students two soft, dull pencils each and tell them to make one clear mark in the answer space, not to waste time neatly filling in circles or spaces.

• Be sure that students understand the difference between a test situation and a cooperative learning situation, in which working with other students is encouraged as an excellent way to learn. In some schools, especially with younger children, the practice of learning together is so ingrained that students have a hard time switching to a situation in which their individual performance is being measured. A clear explanation and a chance to discuss the reasons for individual testing usually enable people to adjust to a test situation.

Suggestions to students

Following are two sets of suggestions to students: first, suggestions for reviewing for tests and exams, and second, suggestions for taking exams and tests based on school courses. Such suggestions can be made orally or in writing and then discussed in class.

Reviewing for Tests and Exams

Reviewing intelligently is an excellent way to learn the material of a course. Don't forget, though, that people's styles of learning differ, so no one system of studying for tests and exams works equally well for everyone. The following suggestions may be helpful, nevertheless.

1. Assemble all your texts, past tests, any notes you have taken, worksheets given out during the course, and a pencil and

paper to make notes as you review.

2. Look over all of the materials you are responsible for mastering. *Don't just reread them.* Remember, you are reviewing, not reading new material for mastery.

    a. Read each heading to see whether you can recall the material that follows. If you can't, read it or skim, if that is enough to recall it to your mind.

    b. Read each underlined or italicized word, each numbered series or list, each item you have marked in any way. Be sure that you understand the significance of all these devices.

    c. Look at all exercises and study questions that may be included to be sure that you do or answer all of them. Understand the reason for each.

    d. Memorize any lists, formulas, or rules you are supposed to know.

3. If you have a great deal of material to review and master, make notes on all main points or items. Then review these notes to see whether you recall the material on which they are based. If you recall little or nothing, reread the material.

4. Review carefully all previous tests, and be sure you can answer all the questions.

5. If you find that you have any questions, write them down and ask them in class, if possible a few days before the test. If some parts seem harder than others, ask the teacher to go over problem areas with you.

6. Try to put yourself in the position of the teacher and think about what kind of test or exam you would give.

7. Just before the test, reread your notes one last time.

8. Sleep long and well the night before the test so that your mind will be fresh.

Taking Tests and Exams

If you can excel in a test or examination, even though you may not have done as well as you'd like in your daily work, you can greatly improve your record. Thinking and writing under pressure, something a test or exam requires, may also be good training for similar challenges in the future. Although test-taking styles differ and people succeed in different ways, the following practices work well for many.

1. Look over the entire test quickly before you start answering any of the questions. Read essay questions right away so that you can mull them over even as you work on other parts of the test. Make short notes on various points to avoid losing ideas you have at first reading.

2. Plan your time. Don't spend more time than you should on any one question. Usually the amount of time allotted to a question is related to the amount of credit given for it. Leave a blank space at the end of each answer in case you have time to come back to it and want to write more.

3. Read the directions and questions carefully to avoid the common pitfall of misinterpreting the directions or answering the wrong question because you have misread it.

4. Write legibly but not too slowly. Never waste time copying over an answer on a timed test.

5. If you don't have an answer sheet, be sure to number your answers according to the numbers of the questions. Make it easy for the teacher to follow your paper.

6. Answer first the questions you know best (but don't spend more than the time allotted on them) and do the hardest ones last — unless, of course, you are required to answer the questions in order.

7. Unless you're an exceptionally good writer, save a few minutes to proofread and revise your answers where needed.

19.
Getting Your
Own Teaching Evaluated

A major complaint of most teachers, both new and experienced, is that they really don't know how well they are doing their jobs, and nobody is willing to tell them. On the other hand, teachers almost universally object to being officially evaluated by their schools, especially if that evaluation is tied to any kind of merit rating that will affect their salaries.

Since this book is mainly for teachers, not administrators, I shall stay away from the sticky question of merit ratings and instead concentrate on how you, a teacher, can get your work evaluated if you really care to do so.

An evaluation questionnaire

One of the best ways to be evaluated, by yourself or by anyone else — including students — is to make up a list of questions about your work and ask people to reply to them. You will certainly find parts of the following set of questions useful, though you will probably need to adapt other parts to your own situation. Clearly, some of the questions are better suited to grade 7 and above than to the elementary grades. Leave space for comments following each question.

Evaluation of _____ (name)

On the line to the right of each question, please rate this teacher from 1 to 5, according to this scale: 1 = Always, 2 = Usually, 3 = Sometimes, 4 = Seldom, 5 = Never. Feel free to use the

space following each question to add whatever comments you wish.

1. Does the teacher have a good knowledge of the subject? _____

2. Is the teacher enthusiastic about the subject? _____
3. Is it clear what the goals of the course are? _____
4. Is the teacher organized and well prepared for class? _____
5. Does the teacher explain the material clearly? _____
6. Is the class flexible enough to allow for unplanned questions that come up in class? _____
7. Does the teacher meet classes regularly? _____
8. Is the teacher on time for classes? _____
9. Is the teacher able to maintain a reasonable level of order and an atmosphere conducive to learning? _____
10. Are deadlines enforced fairly? _____
11. Is the workload (tests, papers, homework) distributed evenly throughout the marking period? _____
12. Are tests and papers returned to the student within a reasonable amount of time? _____
13. Does the teacher respect the students? _____
14. Is the teacher available when students need help? _____
15. Does the teacher show an interest in students' progress and success in the course? _____
16. Does the homework help students learn the subject? _____
17. Is the teacher respected? _____
18. Are the students willing to give the teacher a fair chance? _____

19. Do the students respect one another? _____
20. Do they cut class? _____
21. Are they on time? _____
22. Do the students come to class prepared? _____
23. Do the students participate in class? _____
24. Does the teacher treat the students fairly? _____
25. The tests in this course are

Too hard / Challenging but fair / Adequate / Too easy
1   2   3   4   5

26. The teacher's grading practices are

Fair / Unclear / Unfair
1   2   3   4   5

27. The rate of covering material is

Too fast / Satisfactory / Too slow
1   2   3   4   5

28. List any strong points about the course and the instructor you would like to mention.
29. List any material you feel should be modified or replaced.
30. List any weak points about the course and the instructor and suggestions for improvement.
31. Please feel free to add any other comments you wish to make.

How do you use the answers to a questionnaire like this? Here are some suggestions.

• No matter how good you are, or think you are, be prepared for some shocks. If students answer honestly, there will always be some who will see flaws and suggest improvements. Sometimes the suggestions will be genuine and helpful, sometimes they will be impossible, or born out of a student's own problems and resentments, which may arise from conditions having nothing to do with you or your teaching. I have seen some teachers — good ones — be so shaken and discouraged by the frank opinions of a few of their students that they became less confident, able teachers as a result.

• If you want honest, helpful answers, strongly encourage students not to sign their names.

• Give the questionnaire to any other people — colleagues, administrators, supervisors, assistant teachers — whose opinions you value and ask them to answer those questions on which they have an opinion.

• One of the troubles with most teacher evaluations is that they are done at the end of a course or the year, when nobody can benefit but the teacher and the teacher's new students the following year. I therefore suggest that you use the questionnaire during the school year, not just at the end. Students are most interested in evaluating teaching when they know that something can be done about opinions they express. So as soon as you feel that your students are acquainted with the methods, manner, and content of your teaching, tell them that you'd be helped by a frank evaluation and that you really want their opinions (if they want to give them) to help you plan for the rest of the year. Somewhere around Thanksgiving is the right time, with possibly another, shorter evaluation in February, and then a final one at the end of the year. The one most valuable for you and your students is the Thanksgiving evaluation, since it gives you all plenty of time to use the results.

• Try to find a time to discuss with your classes and any other people who fill out your questionnaire their ratings and opinions. Ask whether they are willing to talk as a group with you about how your teaching might be better and also what they especially like about it. Such a discussion can put comments and recommendations in good perspective and give you a chance to explain why you are teaching what you are teaching and how — both essential to the motivation of most students.

• In discussion, don't be defensive. If you are, you won't get a useful evaluation. Listen, and listen well. Then, if there's something to explain, explain it and ask for reactions to your explanation.

• Take the evaluations of your students seriously, but not with the reverence that should be reserved for profound truth. You may have good reasons for persisting in methods and with materials that your students do not yet appreciate but that they will come to understand and respond favorably to. Don't feel obliged to try to follow every suggestion, even though all should be respectfully considered.

• Every couple of months or so, and especially at midterm and year's end, try to remove yourself from your own teaching and, taking the stance of a tough observer, rate yourself on every item of the questionnaire. After all, you probably know more about your teaching than anyone else.

Other kinds of evaluation

It is probably best for teachers, students, and administrators to devise their own ways and forms for evaluating teacher performance. I therefore won't attempt to give any detailed samples here. Instead, I'd just like to make a few comments about various kinds of evaluation.

One is a general evaluation of a teacher's work, most suitable to be completed by the teacher, the department head or supervisor, colleagues, the principal, and other administrators. Such an evaluation might include questions on a teacher's effectiveness with students, colleagues, and in the life of the school, as well as the teacher's helpfulness and influence in and out of the school. This kind of evaluation forms the basis of a review of a teacher's work when teacher and principal (or other supervisor) meet each year to discuss contract and other arrangements, or simply for a scheduled, thorough evaluative conference. Obviously, this evaluation works best when the teacher completes it, too. And the entire faculty might well discuss its form and content.

An evaluation designed to assess a given unit, short elective course, or even a year-long course is completed by the students themselves. Because students always want to know how the evaluation "came out," it is a good idea, after tabulating the replies, to write out a concise statement of what they contained, what you learned from them, and what changes you expect to make as a result. After reading this to the class for comment, you can share it with a colleague or two, or with your supervisor, department head, or principal, to get their ideas and perspective on the question and to compare their judgment with yours.

Evaluation for lower grades can be somewhat simpler, especially when pupils are involved in the process. Don't forget that even first and second graders can benefit from a chance to express in writing (anonymously) their opinions about what they are doing in school. A simple checklist is probably better than a form that requires a lot of writing. Basically, what you want to know is: What is good? What isn't so good? How do you feel about what goes on? What should be changed?

A few more suggestions

Before moving on to evaluating your school, I have a few final suggestions to offer on evaluating your teaching.

• Invite a colleague or your principal to visit your class. If your experience is like mine, you have had much less visiting and advice than you would like. Often administrators are embarrassed to pop in on your class for fear of making you nervous. If they know that you welcome their visits, they will find it much easier to make them and to be helpful in their comments. When you invite them to visit, ask also that they stay on for a few minutes to discuss what they have observed, if time permits.

• Administrators are often so busy with their own tasks that they are likely to say, with the best intentions, "Sure, I'd be glad to visit your class some time," but just not get around to it. So in addition to expressing a general desire to be visited, occasionally ask for a visit to a specific class, one you expect to be especially interesting or good, or one that you are having problems with and need some advice about.

• Use visitors to your class. If teachers from your school or other schools, or parents, or any other people visit you, give them a chance to express their views on what they see. You can learn a lot, even from untrained observers, and it helps you to keep in touch.

• When you are feeling strong, stand off from your own work and look at it — maybe after an especially good or bad class or day — and ask yourself: What was good? What was bad? Or, as Abbie Hall says, in Hint 53, "Ask yourself 'Would I like to go to school to such a teacher as I am?' "

• Occasionally, when you have a spare moment, ask the class, "Well, how do you think things are going? Any suggestions for me or yourselves?"

• Be sure to look at the standardized test results of your class, both as a group and individual by individual, to see whether by these measures your students are making progress.

• If you have the courage and the equipment is available, have one of your classes videotaped. It can be a real eye opener to see yourself and your students in action. The less of a big deal it can be, the better.

• If there's no way to videotape, get a tape recorder and let it run during an entire class, preferably without telling your students, and then listen critically to the evidence.

• Have a suggestion box so that students can tell you what they think when moved to do so. Steel yourself for the usual number of silly, or even mean, comments that may come along with the valuable ones.

• Take a university or college course or help arrange for an in-service workshop, seminar, or lecture at your school on some basic subject and measure your own work against what you learn. Especially useful, I think, are courses in the psychology of learning, teaching methods, tests and measurement, and your own subject field. Another, easier way to learn and evaluate is for you and a group of colleagues all to read the same book or article and then spend an afternoon or evening discussing it. From such activity often comes excellent evaluation of your teaching and a strong stimulus to do better.

20.
Testing and Evaluating Your School

Before we move on to discussing another aspect of evaluation — marks and comments on papers and report cards — I should say something about the evaluation of an entire school or system of schools.

The true measure of a school

A number of years ago, the head of a well-known independent school spoke to a conference of his fellow school heads and teachers, in whom he found a tendency toward smugness. He said,

> We don't have good schools, we have good students. Our students are so able and highly motivated that they can hardly help succeeding, no matter what their schools are like. The real measure of the excellence of a school is not how many honors its students win when they graduate, or what highly selective colleges they are accepted by, but rather how effectively the school has helped its students to become more highly motivated, more highly skilled, more competent people than they were, and has increased their ability and determination to become good citizens who use the strengths they have to lead more productive and satisfying lives than they would have done had they not attended the school. What has the school done to strengthen the students it enrolls? That is the question.

He went on to point out that many schools that nobody ever praises are probably doing a far better and more difficult job than the selective independent schools, when measured by the amount of improvement they generate rather than by the quality of their graduates. The true measure should be what the school does rather than the quality of students it selects or has fed to it selectively.

Some schools, inspired by excellent principals and flexible, skilled, committed teachers, are able to take on the least promising students and cause them to learn and develop amazingly well — students from broken or single-parent homes, students whose communities neither honor nor exemplify any kind of scholarship, students whose living conditions make it very hard for them to do the sort of reading and writing and thinking and planning that are needed for good schoolwork, students whose parents set few good examples and cannot or do not choose to afford to supply them with the simplest necessities of learning, students who have nothing to look back to with pride and little to look forward to with hope. Schools that work well with students in circumstances like these deserve renown and praise, yet they are seldom heard of.

Measuring a school by standardized test results

It is all too often the style of newspapers and communities to evaluate schools simply by the scores their pupils make on standardized tests: tests of the ability to read, write, spell, and compute — the "basics." People applaud the back to basics, no frills, workbook and drill curriculums that raise those scores.

Well, it is easy enough to raise test scores, but in a way that does little to increase the real skills of students and does not make them, in any lasting way, better readers, writers, spellers, or figurers. The way to do it — and many schools are busy doing it — is to analyze the items on the standardized tests and then drill students on those types of items; teach for the tests, to heck with the rest; teach how to take tests, and teach it over and over; set up special schools that children volunteer to join, so that you get only those students who want to be there and are ready to cooperate, and you are permitted to dismiss those who aren't; require the students to dress according to a code, not to ask probing questions, always to act respectful — and drill, class, drill! If you do that with your school, test scores will go up (in the short run) and you will be praised, even though students' real knowledge and skills will increase only in the narrowest sense.

The only sound way to measure how well a school teaches basic skills is to set as a criterion for success achievement of an acceptable level of competence in skills and to teach for that and beyond. In other words, set a criterion-referenced goal rather than a norm-referenced goal.

If teachers know that their students are to be judged primarily according to results of machine-scored tests, which can measure only the simpler aspects of their subjects, they have little incentive to make their teaching creative and exciting. The students, knowing that the test score is all, turn away from creative use of language, numbers, and concepts.

Evaluating a school on the values it promotes

Earlier, I said that a principal job of schools should be to promote sound values, but that students should never be marked or graded on their values, which are their own business. I think it is desirable, nevertheless, to examine an entire school for values and to make an honest effort to see how well it is promoting them.

The six values I name below are ones that I have found acceptable to almost everyone in a democratic society and that all schools should be encouraged to promote. There's nothing startling about them; in fact, they are so unstartling that we often forget them; but they do provide a good measure for evaluation. Rather than accept these ready-made six, a faculty, or a community, would do well to try to formulate its own statement of values in its own words and then encourage all school people — students, teachers, administrators, and boards of education (or trustees) — to measure their work against these agreed-upon values.

The six values I am about to list were developed during the years I taught the controversial subject called "sex education." I found that publicly basing my teaching and our class discussion on these values, openly stated, increased understanding and acceptance and almost totally ended any opposition. It has since occurred to me that the same values serve as well in any other field of education. Here they are.

1. *Information.* Correct information — the facts — is always

better than ignorance or rumor. Sound information is necessary for sound thinking and responsible action. People get into trouble not because of what they know but because of what they don't know.

2. *Responsibility.* Being responsible means knowing the consequences of what you do — consequences for yourself and for others, present consequences and future consequences. Irresponsibility is the result of not knowing the consequences or of choosing to act without regard for the consequences of your actions.

3. *Control.* Human beings are powerful creatures. We have the power of thought, of language, of muscle, of sex, of invention. We also exercise the power over things we have discovered or made, like fire, automobiles, and weapons. We should be in control of these powers, not let them control us.

4. *Consideration.* In our thoughts and actions, we should be considerate and caring not only of our own needs, feelings, and welfare but of those of others as well. In order to be considerate of others, we need to be able to imagine and put ourselves in their shoes so that we can better try to learn what they may need and want.

5. *Communication.* To be able to exchange ideas, information, and feelings with others is very important. Only thus can we understand one another, and in this way, also, we can test our own ideas. Communication involves both giving and receiving. The skills of communication should have high priority among those things that are taught in schools.

6. *The infinite worth of each person.* To feel the worth of others, we need first to feel our own worth. Self-respect is the beginning of respect for others. The opposite of the feeling of self-worth and respecting the worth of others is expressed by the fifteen-year-old boy who dropped out of school and refused to go back. When asked why, he said, "The teacher looked at me as if I was a nuthin."

A good exercise in evaluation of any school would be for the faculty, or groups of teachers, to sit down together and look hard at their school (not to mention their own work) and its activities — curricular and extracurricular — and to discuss them in the light of the values suggested above. Some questions on the agenda might be these.

Values: Questions for Discussion

1. Do we understand what these values mean? Do we agree with them? Should some be modified or discarded? Do any of them involve imposing values on people against their convictions or will?

2. How do our curriculum and activities strengthen commitment to these values in the lives of our students? Do any aspects of what we do weaken that commitment?

3. What part do our counseling and guidance activities play in developing these values?

4. Can we think of specific incidents, events, programs, comments, and remarks that illustrate in a striking manner the good job or the bad job that our school is doing in developing these values?

5. What changes do we need to make in order to promote these values better?

Evaluating a school on good order, interest, spirit, and discipline

The first four chapters of this book discuss order, interest, spirit, and discipline, all of which can be used to evaluate the work and life of a school. Why not have the faculty (or a group of the faculty) read one of the first four chapters of this book? Then discuss the chapter and its suggestions, always in relation to the school's own realities.

Ask five members of the group to form a panel to start the discussion, and ask each panel member to be prepared to explain two or three specific ways in which the school is especially good or poor in developing good order, interest, spirit, or discipline — whichever one is the topic. Then open the discussion to all, or break up into small discussion groups, to try to agree on ways in which the school is doing a good job and ways in which it could do better.

Some additional suggestions

Here are some more suggestions involving teachers and others in the school as well as outsiders in the evaluation of the school.

● Schools tend to evaluate only new programs, courses, or

activities, but not the old, tried, and perhaps true. At times, a school should call up for evaluation the most firmly established aspects of its work and program in the same way that every item is scrutinized in zero-based budgeting.

• Be careful of excessively favorable evaluations of new programs, whose success may spring principally from the creative energy of experiment. As someone said, "All educational experiments are doomed to succeed."

• It can be useful to take a major area of a school and have the entire school look critically at it. The area can be a subject or skill (reading, mathematics, foreign language, science, physical education) or a grade or set of grades (grades 4-6, kindergarten and grade 1, the eighth grade, senior year). Such an evaluation can be enlightening both for those who work directly in the activity, who need an independent, outside look at what they are doing, and for those who know little about the activity in question and whose teaching may be enriched by what they learn about another aspect of the school.

• You as a teacher can be helpful in initiating the evaluation of your school by making an appointment to talk with the principal or other person in authority about any area that concerns you and that you think needs to be evaluated. Most administrators welcome teachers who bring fundamental questions to them rather than immediate crises, and they are likely to take up your concern and help work out plans for evaluation. One thing to remember, though, is that administrators, who have the unenviable responsibility for seeing to it that everything goes well — or at least looks as if it were — are much more likely to be receptive to an evaluation proposal that is presented in a constructive way than to one presented in a way that is likely to turn it into a mere exchange of gripes. Nothing is much worse than a group gripe session. Emphasis should be on what's good, what needs to be improved, and, specifically, how it can be improved.

• One of the most common methods of evaluating schools, especially independent schools whose accreditation by regional and state associations is reconsidered periodically, is evaluation by a committee of one's peers and associates from other schools, both private and public, often helped by selected specialists from universities. Probably the most important part of this evaluation process is the self-evaluation that a faculty performs before the visit of the committee. This self-evaluation is usually based on a far-reaching, many-paged set of forms filled out by individuals and various departments, with self-ratings given. Then the committee comes and, in two or three days of intense activity, looks closely at the school and at its self-evaluation, then draws up lists of commendations and recommendations. The trouble with these evaluations is that they too often become exercises in mutual back scratching, with the result that hard, honest, valuable criticism is rarely given. Another trouble is that the school being evaluated undergoes a flurry of painting and cleaning; the bulletin boards flower with evidence of creativity; the teachers are on their best behavior and use their best lesson plans; and the students, rising to the occasion, are bright, eager, well prepared, and cordial. The committee's tour through the school is a little like Catherine the Great's trip through southern Russia in 1787, with false housefronts in "Potemkin villages" hiding the crumbling structures behind, and specially dressed, cheerful peasants lining the streets, and the miserable majority kept well out of sight as the empress's carriage passed through.

• If a school wants a really honest, helpful, objective, professional, independent evaluation, it should ask an outside person well versed in the area that needs evaluating to come in for visits, conversations, and then an oral report to and discussion with the faculty, followed by a written report.

• No matter who comes — a committee of peers or an outside expert — the school will be served best if it tries to show its ordinary good and bad self, unvarnished, and if its leaders make it clear that what they want is sound opinions, not flattery. Unfortunately, many school people are loath to admit that anything they do is not working well.

21.
Marks and Comments

> *Hint 22.* No teacher should be continually saying to his pupils, "You will surely fail on examination with such lessons as these," "You are doing poorly," etc. It irritates both pupil and teacher.   *Abbie G. Hall*

I've been talking about evaluating the performance of students, teachers, and schools. Now I return to students and one of the most stark and controversial forms of evaluation: marks. It is a subject on which there are more closed minds than on almost any other aspect of education.

In the 1960's and middle 1970's, much was written against using marks, and a number of forward-looking schools and colleges abandoned grading systems and turned to pass/fail plans. Even at the height of the pass/fail wave, however, only a minute fraction of schools and colleges gave up some sort of traditional marking system, and when pass/fail was presented to students as an option rather than a requirement, only a small minority chose it, except in physical education and performance courses like music and art, in which it is common for schools to require a no-mark evaluation. People who oppose marks are intelligent and persuasive, and they may yet gain the day, but I doubt it.

The arguments against giving marks

The case against marks, and the research studies that back them up, are convincingly assembled in a lively little book called *Wad-ja-get? The Grading Game in American Education*, by Howard Kirschenbaum, Rodney Napier, and Sidney B. Simon (New York: Hart, 1971). Its arguments, as follows, are not easily dismissed.

1. Marks increase competition and sometimes set one student at war with another.

2. Marks cause cheating (most students in high school and college admit to cheating).

3. Marks are inaccurate measures of performance, mean different things in different schools, to different teachers in the same school, and even to the same teacher at different times.

4. Marks provide extraneous motivation and thus stifle love of learning.

5. Marks push teachers into emphasizing gradable content in nicely packaged sets of academic goods that are easily measured and not creative.

6. Marks discourage originality and risk taking on the part of students, encourage parroting, and measure the power of automatic answer giving.

7. Marks spoil teacher-pupil relations by setting teacher against pupil. *Wad-ja-get?* quotes a school consultant on this point: "Each enemy is equipped with vicious weapons. The student has his crib sheets, his ponies, his apple-polishing, rote memorization, fawning obsequiousness, and other kinds of con-artistry. On our side, we teachers resort to micky mouse assignments, surprise quizzes, unannounced notebook checks, tricky multiple-choice questions, and irrelevant essay questions." (p. 163)

8. Marks spoil the joy of working.

9. Marks are undemocratic and divisive.

10. Marks are an obstacle to the development of one's self as a person.

11. Marks encourage those who need it least and discourage those who are most in need of encouragement.

12. And, anyway, marks are a relatively recent development, having become common only around the turn of the century, when some sort of easy selection and sorting process was necessary, all the way from the professional schools down into the grade schools.

The arguments in favor of giving marks

So what's to be said *for* marks? Very much, and most people in schools and colleges are persuaded by the arguments. Here they are.

1. Marks do motivate students to work. Perhaps they shouldn't but they do, and not all work in school can be made continuously interesting enough to provide steady motivation without them.

2. Marks provide clear, unemotional, graspable pieces of information. For example, some students do not "hear" an unfavorable comment on a report, but they do hear a D. I know many guidance and counseling people who insist that children who have no realistic vision of their deficiencies be given regular, even weekly, marks. One boy in a no-mark elementary school was not doing well in his work, and the school psychologist prescribed weekly marks in each "subject." The boy was flabbergasted when he got C's and D's. He had filtered out all the "bad" no-mark comments and thought he was an A student. Psychiatrists, too, tend to recommend more, not less, "reality" and hard evidence of reality for children who have problems.

3. Most students want marks so that they can know where they stand (but not on a rank list).

4. Marks provide the quick information about their work that most students need and like. David McClelland, a psychology professor at Harvard, has some original ideas about marks. He has especially studied people's motivation to achieve and motivation to exercise power. He says that people who are highly motivated to achieve do not really need marks, for their satisfaction comes from their own knowledge that they have learned. But if the marks provide a reasonably valid measure of learning, achievement-oriented students are helped by them. The situation is somewhat different for people highly motivated to exercise power, who pay attention to what the world expects of them. They very much want marks, which they see as clear stamps of approval that can be exhibited and used to climb to success. McClelland says that recent tests of his show that American society has now entered a strongly power-oriented phase, whereas a decade or two ago we were more oriented toward achievement. Grades, he says, prepare you to do better in a power-oriented society. He stresses the importance of regular evaluation of all students' work if they are to improve.

5. Teachers want to give marks and believe it is helpful to tell students where they stand.

6. Marks give teachers a convenient, workable system of record keeping that lets them know where each student stands, how he is progressing, and what he needs in the way of special work and help.

7. Marks stimulate students to ask, "How can I do better?" and "What are the goals of this course, and how do you measure me against them?" which are good questions. Most teachers usually know what they're doing — despite claims to the contrary — can explain it to their students, and are able to measure the results over the long run of a school year, usually with a healthy leaven of doubt.

8. Finally, marks do provide a workable means of transfer from school to school and to college and professional school for those who want to go.

If marks, at what age should they start?

Clearly, no sensible person advocates marks in kindergarten and first grade, so when do we start marking? In the early grades, schools tend, rightly, to keep the kids "awash with encouragement." They need immediate evaluation, but in forms more concrete than a mark.

Fifth grade, or possibly fourth, is about the right time to begin marks and comments, I think. By age nine or ten, most girls and boys have reached a pleasant state of adjustment. They tend to feel as secure about themselves as they ever will; most of them can read, write, and figure; they like life, school, and teachers; and they like acquiring information and skills. They are pleasantly realistic and ready for realism. And I think they are ready to be introduced to the full marking system of the school they are in, whatever that system may be. It is not necessary to ease them gradually into the idea of marks. It's not so hard to understand.

What system of marks works best?

I know of a college that gave students marks like 97− or 84+, and of a school where poems received marks like 83.4. To me, such "precise" marks are no more valid or reliable than the result announced by the person who paces off a room and then, as he approaches the wall, gets out a micrometer to measure the last bit to the nearest millimeter.

I have never understood how a student's performance could be marked 72 instead of 73 on a scale of 60 to 100. You just can't make 40 degrees of differentiation unless, of course, you simply mark by the percent right and then average all the marks to get the final grade — a ridiculous sort of exercise. The only advantage I can see for such spuriously refined gradations is that they appear to be objective, and their utterly unchallengeable arithmetic saves the teacher from having to explain, argue, or think.

The two chief characteristics of a sound marking system are that it does not make unrealistically fine distinctions and that its terms or symbols are clearly defined or explained, with no delusions of infallibility. Most schools have a well-established marking system, published and explained on report cards and elsewhere.

Regardless of your convictions or preferences, I think the best policy — assuming that you have any choice — is to understand fully and to adopt the system your school uses, and to be sure that your students understand it. Remember, however, that to put great emphasis on marks is distracting from the main business of education — which is to teach good, useful skills, information, habits, values, and attitudes toward oneself, others, the community, and the world. The emphasis should be that the purpose of marks is to convey information that will help students to further learning. Marks should not be considered symbols to compete for.

Here is an example of a marking system that works well for a good many schools: A and A— = excellent, B+ = very good, B = good, B— = fairly good, C+ and C = fair, C— = barely fair, D = poor, and NC = no credit (or BMS = below minimum standard). Whatever system is used, I suggest not using the common mark F for "failing" because it is such a heavy term and may connote failure as a person in addition to failure of work. If your school does use F (and F does convey a strong message that many teachers feel is useful and educational), take special care to see that your students know that it refers to their work, not to them.

It is important, too, for everyone to understand that C for

"fair" does not mean "average." In most schools where the work means something, the teaching is good, and the students are well motivated, the average (most frequently given) mark should be in the "good" range. In a school that has unmotivated, antagonistic students, routine, dull, imposed work, and tired, overburdened teachers who use heavy, dated, inflexible materials, most marks may be "fair" and below.

It is a sad thing that in many schools, especially those in crowded urban areas, most marks are in the "poor" to "failing" range. A number of large school systems have even resorted to marking for several degrees of failure — almost like saying "failing," "very failing," "superfailing," and "hopelessly failing." Probably such schools should give up marks altogether and consider a radical shift of teaching methods, class organization, and instructional materials.

Marks and comments

One great trouble with marks, especially those given to students to evaluate their work on a long paper (or a unit or a whole year's work) is that so many factors, elements, and judgments get summed up and set down in a single symbol: B−, C, A. What does the C mean? Well, if the course has been a good one, with continuing communication between teacher and student, the meaning of C may be clear to the student. But will it be clear to the student's parents? Almost certainly not, beyond the definition published — in the case of C, "fair." But what kind of "fair"?

It might mean a student who is dutiful and careful and whose work is mechanically correct but who lacks originality and depends largely on the teacher's organization and presentations. Or a student whose work is marred by serious mechanical errors but who demonstrates fairly good comprehension of the main ideas of the course. Or a very able student who produces little, whether because of laziness, disorganization, or other compelling interests.

A student who gets a B is "good," but what kind of "good"? This student might be a brilliant person who is working somewhat sloppily or not at full effort. Or a person of only moderate ability who is working at full capacity. Or a person whose ideas and concepts are exceptionally good but who has trouble with mechanical errors and detail.

If there is to be enlightened communication about papers, projects, units, and courses, marks must be accompanied by comments. In the next chapter, I talk about reports and report cards, and in the chapter after that I make some suggestions about marking and dealing with papers written by students. Let me give a few examples here, however, of the kinds of good comments that help to illuminate a mark or set of marks on report cards.

B   Julius spells well, punctuates carelessly; content of written work excellent. Should read more and better books. Excellent discusser when attentive, but too often I have to compel his attention.

D   Despite the D, I don't think Josie's situation is hopeless. Her last two papers were fair, and she seems to be learning from her extra sessions. Must be more careful about mechanics.

C   Jack has an able mind, which he is not using well. His computation is careless and his assignments often are late and poorly done. Does well on tests, however.

D   This is a hard subject for Jim. His memory for sounds is poor, and he seems discouraged. Often he is not attentive. I am giving him extra help. I think a conference is called for.

A   A delight to teach! Betsy's extra project on worms was excellent. Daily work shows creativeness.

Note that none of these comments says anything about the student's quality as a person. All of them focus on performance, all are factual, and, where needed, either make a suggestion for improvement or indicate that help is being provided. None says, in effect, "A hopeless child whom I can't seem to teach or control." If that's actually the case, write something ambiguous and get help.

In the following samples of comments on papers, no marks are shown here, though these papers would be marked — a mark for content, a mark for spelling, and a mark for mechanics.

This held my interest and I chuckled over the ending. I have starred three places that should have been more fully developed.

Read your papers *aloud* to catch run-on sentences!

Good beginning; confusing ending — please rewrite last page. How much time did you spend on this? *See me.*

I think you didn't spend enough effort on this to make it work marking. *Redo.*

Very well put together, but your evidence is very slight. Give more examples to support your statements.

You report your facts clearly, but what are your conclusions? What did you set out to show? Be clear about your purpose before you start.

Some further suggestions

Here are some further suggestions about marks and comments.

• In order to see how fallible you are, try grading a set of papers twice, not writing on them the first time and recording your marks on a separate place. If you can do so (though usually you shouldn't keep papers this long), let a week or ten days go by between markings.

• To save time on comments, if you have many students, a heavy schedule, and thus little time for writing comments, give marks for effort (making it clear that this is only your impression), for classroom conduct, for promptness in turning in work, and even — if sloppiness is a widespread problem — for neatness of work.

• Never mark students on their ability, only on their performance. Some teachers give students good marks just because they're bright. Others give low marks for the same reason if the performance is only good but not as good as they think it should be. A mark should be based on a standard of performance. Students have a right to know where their performance stands in relation to an external standard of measurement.

• Be cautious about giving an unrealistically high mark because you think a student needs encouragement. This practice is likely to backfire next time.

• It's not a bad idea to use different marking systems at different times, merely to force students to ask, again, "What does this mark mean?"

• For very special work a student may be required to do and

for which you really don't want to give a conventional mark and yet need some kind of indication in your record book, since you consider the task involved an important part of the total work (for example, a freely written daily journal), devise a special, absolutely nonthreatening set of symbols, such as RS = really something, S = something, NM = not much, as far as I can tell, and N = nothing, as far as I can tell. At least that way you'll have some kind of record in your book when the time comes to evaluate a student's total performance.

• If the question "Wad-ja-get?" circulates feverishly around the classroom when papers, tests, or reports are handed back, be ready to answer, "That's the wrong question. Ask yourself what the marks and comments tell *you* about *your* work. Remember, marks are information. Use them as such."

22.
Reports to Parents and Students

> *Hint 70.* Try to send the children home with favorable reports of your work as a teacher. Don't despise these little advertisements if deserving.   *Abbie G. Hall*

Obviously, at least in the upper grades, marks and comments are closely linked to reports. Please keep in mind and refer to the facts and opinions in the preceding chapter as you read this one.

Reports sent home in middle and upper grades

Probably your school has an established form for making reports to students and their parents. Be sure you understand how it works and how you are supposed to use it. Also, be sure that your students and their families understand it.

If marks are given, a good report form will include the definition of each mark. If it doesn't, write the definitions on the board or enclose a duplicated slip with the report so that all concerned will understand what each symbol means.

When you write comments on a report sent home, it is wise to stick to the facts. It is also pointless to say, "Very good work," when a B+ already says that. Perhaps "Nice going, John," will make John feel good, but it's even better to tell him what is so good. Worse is, "You can do better, John," or "You should do better," without any suggestion of how he should do better. Most good reports say something encouraging and add a suggestion or two about how the student can improve.

The customary purpose of a report is to give an account of the status and progress of the student in your subject. It should enlighten the student and the parents about his or her strengths and weaknesses in the subject, and also, perhaps, as a member of the class. It should suggest how the student can do better. If the subject is one involving basic skills (reading, writing, computation, logical thinking, organization), at some time early in the year you should report on the state of these skills insofar as you have evidence about them. Be sure to look at last year's reports first to make sure that you are not reporting, without recognizing and explaining it, something quite different from what last year's teacher said. You may also want to say something about how these skills show themselves in class and schoolwork as compared to the measures on standardized tests, but it is best, as I have said, not to give actual test scores.

You should avoid several pitfalls when writing reports, as follows.

• Don't play psychiatrist. Leave deep analysis of the student's character or family and other relationships to counselors and specialists. If something concerns personal or family adjustment, it's better to talk about it in a conference than in writing. In a written report, stick to observed facts, from which the parents and student can draw conclusions, perhaps with your help. Stick to what you know.

• Avoid a tone of cleverness or even humor. Reports are usually taken very seriously by those who read them, and if you sound light and witty rather than factual, you run a danger. Especially avoid sarcasm. I remember once writing about an amiable, popular, lazy sixth grader, "Paul is filled with love, but love is not enough." This was true, but Paul's mother still quotes it to me as a piece of irreverence they did not appreciate.

• Don't predict. By saying, "I am sure Sally will do much better during the next marking period," you may mean to encourage Sally, but when she doesn't do better, you are left in an awkward position. Why doesn't she do better? Probably because you haven't taught her properly. It's better to say, "Sally can do better, I think, and here are a few suggestions . . ."

• If in doubt when writing the first report of the year, mark on the low side but make your comments as encouraging and constructive as possible. It's much better to be able to report improvement as the year goes on than to have to back away from an unsound judgment made earlier. Some students do go downhill during the year for reasons that may be entirely beyond your control, so if Polly is having a midwinter slump, report that fact to her parents and to her.

• Don't write comments that make you sound ineffectual, like, "I just don't know what to do about Billy's talking in class," or "How can we teach Mary not to hand in so many late papers?" The parents will probably say, frustrated, "Well, what are we supposed to do about it? That's your job." It's better to say, "Billy has to learn to control himself in class so that I won't have to. I've made some suggestions to him," or "For the past two weeks I've been keeping Mary after school when she hands her papers in late. I hope she will soon learn to meet deadlines."

• Don't put off pointing out a weakness or a problem that may cause trouble later in the year, like inability to do simple arithmetic, a very slow reading rate, or inability to concentrate for more than a few minutes. Parents want and students need to know about such fundamental problems early so that they and the school can tackle them as soon as possible. Many a parent has been justifiably disaffected and many a child put at a disadvantage by teachers' unfounded hopes that problems will simply be outgrown without attention or help. Often they are, and then everyone is happy, but if they aren't, time is wasted. A benign early warning policy is valuable.

• If reports are handed out to students as a group, don't allow a frantic, whispered round of "Wad-ja-get?" Too many students feel hurt, embarrassed, and helpless in such situations. Instead, be sure to tell students that people have the right to keep their reports private and that reports are used for giving information, not for comparing. Take enough time to discuss this so that students really understand and accept it and then strictly enforce the no-comparing rule while the students are in your room. What happens outside you cannot control.

• Even though reports are addressed to parents and are to be taken home and shown to Mom and Dad, probably their most important function is what they say to the student: "Al, your work since January . . ." No matter to whom addressed, the message should be one that will be helpful to the student, who should not be talked about as if he or she were an absent, nonreading entity.

• Sometimes it is useful to hand out reports to students at a time when each can discuss his briefly with you while the rest of the class work independently at their desks. In this way, any obvious misunderstandings can be cleared up before the reports go home. It's best to let students read their reports first and then to ask those who wish to do so to talk with you briefly. If it's clear that a long conference will be needed, schedule it for later so that all who need it can have at least a moment to raise their brief questions. If you are quite sure that some students will be too shy to ask to see you, you had better ask to see them.

• If one isn't provided, make a copy for yourself of what you have written about each student in case you need it for reference or later conference purposes.

• Don't make the mistake of thinking that the mark on a final report for the year must be some sort of average of the marks and reports for all the grading periods or units during the year. In cumulative subjects like math and languages, but also in English, history, and science, the most important question to consider at the end of the year is, "How competent is this student to do work in this subject now, after all the ups and downs of the year?" (I'm convinced that you *do* history or science or English; you don't memorize them or store them up in unit-size, labeled morsels.) If Sarah started poorly in social studies, wrote miserable papers, didn't know how to plan her time, was silent or disruptive in class, and failed some tests on the first two units out of six in the year but ended up as a fine class member, a good essay writer, a competent learner and thinker, and showed that she had mastered the problem of planning her time, she should certainly get an A or a B despite those D's near the beginning.

• Encourage parents to respond to their children's reports. Either by being able to reply in writing on the report or in a conference, they can give you insights that may help you teach their children better.

• It's not a bad idea to encourage, but not require, students to write a response to their reports. It stimulates them to think about what your report said, and it may give you helpful reactions. Some teachers ask students to write their own reports and give themselves marks before they write the students' reports. This is another way to get students to think about their attitudes, performance, and aptitudes.

Reports about younger children

Much of what I have written about reports for the middle and upper grades also applies to the lower grades and kindergarten. Since it is likely that no marks will be given until fourth or fifth grade, many schools and teachers prefer, at least during the first half of the school year, to have conferences instead of sending a written report home. One danger of not making a written report, though, is that parents will not "hear" what you are telling them about their children, and no record of it will exist in case problems come up later and parents complain that "nobody ever told us." Perhaps it is best, therefore, to have a written report accompany your oral report to parents.

In a conference, it is helpful to have a checklist to make sure that nothing really important is forgotten. On the other hand, you don't have to go slavishly over every item on the list just because it's there. It is obviously better to concentrate on particular points that apply to the student being discussed.

Below, I suggest some headings that you might want to include on your checklist, a copy of which both you and the parents can have before you while you talk. You can fill in the details as they fit your school's situation. By keeping the list informal, you will help to put parents at ease and in the mood to talk.

Checklist for Parent-Teacher Conference

1. Any outstanding problems or concerns — of parents, teachers, child?

2. How about the child's basic skills and attitudes toward them — in reading, writing, math (arithmetic), speaking, discussing, study skills?

3. How about other schoolwork (various subjects), homework (if any), and motivation in general?

4. Any home problems that interfere with school, or vice versa?

5. How about recreation and free time?

6. Other home matters?

7. How about health and physical considerations?

8. Social adjustment?

9. Personality?

10. Any problems we agreed on? Follow-up action? Anything special to tell the child? If so, who to do the telling? Should we meet again?

Here are two last, very important points about parent conferences.

• Do your best to be honest, to stick to what you know, and not to make things look better or worse for the student or for the school than they are.

• Never blame parents. Parents almost always try as hard as they can, perhaps against odds and forces you know nothing about, and they don't need blaming. Never let your words or voice take on a threatening tone, either.

Parent-teacher conferences at any level

I have been in many parent-teacher conferences, often as parent, more often as teacher, where time was wasted or poorly used. Here are some suggestions that might help overcome that problem.

• Remember that a student is one person but that his life is divided into at least two parts: home and school. If you and the parents can work together, the student is likely to benefit. Therefore, if possible, at least through eighth grade, teachers should try to confer with the parents of each student at least once a year to see how things are going.

• Ask parents to call school for an appointment. A well-organized school will leave a message for you, and you can return the call when you're free. If parents happen to run into you and want to talk right then, feel perfectly free to say you're busy just then and ask whether they can talk to you at a specified time.

• When parents want to see you, encourage them to tell you ahead of time what they especially want to talk about so that you can prepare to be as helpful as possible.

• Plunge right into the subject of the conference. It is tempting to ease into things by talking about the weather or politics or the recent school play instead of spending time on what the parents really want to talk about. Make a point of saying, almost right away, "Well, let's see, we're going to talk about Bob's difficulty in math," or "Do you want to start with your questions about Julie, or shall I talk about a couple of things we have on our minds?"

• Remember that most school problems are rather compli-

cated, and simple answers are not likely to be useful. Therefore, be cautious when a parent says, "I only need five minutes
of your time." It is almost certain to take longer; if you don't
allow more time, both you and the parents will leave unsatis-
fied. Once a mother saw me in the hall, asked for "just five
minutes," sat down with a sigh, and said, "We are convinced
our daughter can't spell and doesn't understand what she's
reading. What should we do?"

• Often, it can be more helpful to include the student in the
conference than to talk about him or her in absentia. When
students aren't present, it means that parents or teachers must
explain later what went on, perhaps not as accurately or impres-
sively as letting the student hear it all in the first place. If
students are present, they can't play teacher and parent off
against each other. Also, many students feel that it isn't quite
fair for adults — even loving, intelligent ones — to talk about
them when they aren't there. They may not need or want to
defend themselves, but often right in the conference they can
do some helpful explaining and expressing of feelings. If the
student is to be there, parents or teachers must not act or seem
to act as a powerful double hammer of authority. The student
needs a chance to talk and explain and react. Of course, it is
obviously more appropriate for a ninth grader to be at a conference than for a fourth grader. Also, there are feelings (anger,
deep discouragement, distrust) and topics (the methods used by
a teacher, fundamental objections to the school, suspected
need for psychiatric evaluation or treatment) that are better
discussed, at least in the early stages, without the student
present.

General grade meetings of parents

An excellent and efficient way to get in touch with parents and
keep them informed about their children's lives, about school,
and about what and how you are teaching is to call a meeting of
all the parents of a grade, as early in the year as you have
learned most of the names of your students and a little about
them — which probably means the middle of October. These
meetings, whose tone should be kept informal but not careless,
can be presided over by the principal, grade head, or a teacher

who is good at this kind of thing. In preparing your presentation, you might consider the following ideas.

● Explain clearly and specifically what you hope to teach the students this year and how you expect to go about it.

● Tell parents how they can help. If the best help is for them to do nothing, so that you can know how well the students are working and thinking entirely on their own, say so.

● Unless the school discourages it, or unless it makes you uncomfortable, invite parents to visit your class whenever they wish to. Usually they won't, but they like to feel they can, and when they do it's almost always beneficial.

● Be careful not to claim that "this grade" is "*the* crucial, watershed year" of a student's education. This may be true, but it probably isn't, and when parents hear teacher after teacher say it year after year, they get skeptical. Just tell them why what you're doing is important and what you hope your students will accomplish.

● After all the teachers have spoken, invite parents to ask questions, but ask them to stick to questions of general interest to everyone.

● Say whether you are or are not willing to be called at home and under what, if any, circumstances. Some teachers enjoy telephone conferences, which can be extremely useful.

● Explain, or ask someone else to explain, that usually when children go from one grade to another they have new teachers, and that some of the successful methods worked out with previous teachers may not have been communicated to the new teachers. Although your school may have faculty meetings early each year where the teachers of each grade share their ideas and experiences in working with individual students, even important matters like this are sometimes overlooked. It is therefore helpful for parents to write a note early in the year to the homeroom teacher or some other person who is in touch with their child's teachers if there is any point that they particularly want not to be forgotten — "Please be sure to seat Barry near the front of the room, where he can see the board, because he won't sit there unless you ask him to," or "Maud had math tutoring all summer. If she seems to need more, we'd like to know right away. It got her through quite well last year."

23.
Dealing with the
Written Work of Students

Hint 7. Train your older pupils to correct and
credit the papers of younger ones.
Abbie G. Hall

In this chapter, I come even farther out of the closet, and my
biases as a teacher of English are starkly revealed. I think every
teacher is a teacher of English, or should be, and that the writing of English that is good, clear, and appropriate to its purpose
involves a set of skills and attitudes we all should be working
on.

I will admit that every teacher also should be a teacher of
science and history and art and morals and math, which is just
another way of saying that knowledge and feelings don't divide
up very well into compartments. But the most important subject for everybody to be a teacher of is English, and especially of
reading and writing. Reading is too complicated to discuss at
length here, except that I urge you to keep teaching that there
is more than one way to read (see Chapter 5) and to be alert to
those students who can't read well enough and try to get expert
help for them.

Correcting and editing papers

One extraordinary phenomenon, the learn-it-my-way idiocy, is
the failure of most schools — including every one I have ever
taught in — to establish, by edict or consensus, a common set
of symbols and a single system of editing and "correcting"
written work. Instead, each teacher has his or her own favorite
system, and each pupil has to learn the different systems
teacher by teacher, year by year.

Let there be one system; let all learn it and operate it — the English department, the history department, the biology department, the math department. And let it start with a few elements in the first grade and develop with splendid uniformity and increasing but always consistent complexity through to the twelfth grade. The alternative is time wasted, papers inefficiently corrected, and corrections misunderstood or not understood by students.

It doesn't matter exactly what the system is, as long as it is sensible and has some relation to symbols commonly used in the great outside world of writing. (I suggest one such system in my book *How To Achieve Competence in English: A Quick-Reference Handbook,* published in paperback by Bantam in 1976.)

Some suggestions about correcting and editing papers

There are some ways of going about correcting and editing papers that work better than others. Here they are.

• Unless you are an English teacher, you probably don't have enough time to deal thoroughly with all written work, but do your best, and don't let anyone get away with the "Oh, but I thought punctuation only counted in English papers" fallacy.

• Don't swamp a paper with correction marks so that it looks more like a disease than a piece of edited writing. "Correct" and comment on only as much as you think the student can deal with and not be discouraged. This means letting some errors pass, at least this time.

• Don't be so preoccupied with simple mechanical errors (which you can learn to correct without much thought) that you do not give attention to larger and more important matters like content, word choice, organization, and tone.

Evaluating student writing

I think it is useful to give all important papers three marks: one for content (what the paper says, by far the most important mark), one for spelling (the least important, except for the real and unfortunate prejudice our society has in favor of correct spelling and people's mistaken belief that spelling and intelligence correlate), and one for mechanics (capitalization, punctuation, and indications of organization — paragraphs, etc.). These three aspects of writing are quite, though not entirely, discrete and thus should be marked separately. A single mark is as meaningless as the "Total" figure on a sign outside an apocryphal town, reading, "You are entering Jenksburg. Established: 1832. Altitude: 735. Population: 4,321. Total: 6,888."

If a student, looking at the paper and seeing "Content = B+, Spelling = C−, Mechanics = A" says, "Yes, but what did the paper *get*?" You should answer, "It got three pieces of informed judgment that should provide you with some useful information." Then add, "If you read the comment I wrote at the top and all of the editings and corrections I put in the margins, you will have learned something valuable about how well you write and how to write better."

Persuading students to revise and correct their papers

The best motivation is persuasion backed by requirement. When you hand back a batch of papers, you might make the following speech or something like it.

> When I give your paper back, you will probably need to revise it, to "correct it," because writing should be a *process of improvement*, not setting down a fixed thing, getting it marked, and then going on to the next thing. It's like practicing any sport. If a move or a play goes wrong, the coach will probably say, "That's wrong. Here's how you should have done it," and then tell the players to go over it again so they'll learn to *do it right.*
>
> When you write a paper, you usually make some errors in spelling, punctuation, capitalization, and sentence structure, no matter how carefully you have gone over it. In most cases, I have suggested changes, perhaps in sequence and organization, development of ideas, need to strengthen the argument, clearing up fuzzy ideas, and eliminating needless repetition. Benefit from these corrections and suggestions; they are directed specifically at you. Revise your paper and make all the corrections; in other words, "Do it right." Very often people learn more from revising a paper than from first writing it. The time I've spent on each of these papers is like individual tutoring that you might have to

pay $10 or $15 an hour for. So get the most out of what I've tried to show you as I read and edited your papers.

Even better than a speech is a discussion during which the class figures out for itself the benefits of correcting and revising papers.

A system for correcting and revising papers

Require that students correct and revise their papers after you have marked and commented on them. Here is a system that works.

1. Explain why papers must be corrected.

2. Require that papers be revised and corrected and handed in the next day, or, if there is much other work going on, by another close deadline. (A lot more learning occurs when things are fresh in everyone's mind.)

3. Require that every correction signal and revision suggestion you have made be dealt with and the paper returned to you for rechecking, and keep up this exchange until you OK the paper for filing.

4. Mark the corrections and revisions, perhaps thus: OK = job completed, file the paper; + = good job, but some items still need to be dealt with; 0 = fair job, more to be done; − = poor job, more to be done.

To you and your students, this may at first seem like a lengthy, complicated system, but once it is learned and its operation made routine, it works quickly and is an effective way of improving the writing of your students.

Some shortcuts in dealing with papers

No matter how fast, bright, expert, and decisive you may be, if you have five classes a day and 100 pupils or more and are having your students write more than once every two weeks or so, you're going to have to use some shortcuts. They may not be the ideal way to deal with writing, but they are better than nothing at all. Here they are.

• Anticipate difficulties and preteach. Having already dealt with this subject in Chapter 10, on homework, I need only remind you that papers that are written better because of writing problems foreseen and solved in advance are much more quickly read and marked than those that are full of errors and inadequacies that could have been avoided.

• Make specific, short assignments. By making your assignments very specific so that the class understands exactly what it is supposed to do and why, you will be able to determine quickly, when it comes to marking the papers, whether or not the assignment has been adequately done. Nothing is more time consuming than marking a set of papers written on "anything you want."

• Sometimes, read aloud and edit papers in class. Have a cross section of students read their papers aloud, or you read them aloud. Stop after every three or four papers to deal then and there with the most evident errors, weaknesses, strengths, and gems on the board and in discussion. Be careful not to be hard on papers written by timid souls. You may allow students to take some class time to improve their papers in the light of what they're hearing. Then take in the papers, glance at them, and either throw them away (because they have performed their teaching function) or put a check at the top of each to show that you have seen it and hand them all back with a short spoken comment to the entire class the next day but with no further reading.

• Base a lesson on common writing problems. Scan an entire set of papers, making no marks on them, but pick out five or six important common problems and then teach a lesson based on these problems the very next day. Before teaching the lesson, hand back the papers so that the students can evaluate and revise their own work in relation to the points being discussed.

• Teach from sentences written on the board or duplicated. Read enough papers to find out what the important problems are. Then underline or star certain sentences and passages on certain papers. The next day, ask the students whose papers you have marked to write the starred or underlined passage on the board *as is*, and use these sentences as the basis for the lesson. If possible, it works even better to duplicate these passages and give a copy to each student. You can also project items, if an overhead projector is available and their authors don't object.

• Have students form groups to read and react. Small groups provide a means for each pupil to read his or her paper to others and have their reactions to it — a most important aspect of evaluation. Discuss in advance what students should be listening for as they hear the papers, and write some items on the board — "interesting beginning," "good description," "awkward repetitions" — to listen for and to discuss. Students can even evaluate one another's papers if no one objects.

• Read a cross section of papers aloud and then have students revise their own papers. On the basis of a quick scan the day before, pick out two very good ones, two mediocre ones, and two poor ones, and read them to the class, discussing and criticizing as you read. Ask students to take notes on the discussion. Then hand all of the papers back, unmarked, and have the students examine and revise their own papers in light of the discussion. This method works especially well when the same topic has been assigned to all students and they can compare the different methods of dealing with the question.

• "Correct" or edit only part of long papers. If students are doing long papers, it is sometimes all right to correct carefully and completely only the first two or three pages for spelling and mechanics and to read the remaining pages without making detailed corrections. (From time to time, correct only the last two pages.) Be sure, though, to make comments and suggestions about style, organization, and content that cover the entire paper.

• Under some circumstances, simply return some sets of papers unread. If you are convinced that the main value of an assignment was the doing of it, if you have more important planning or tasks to do, or if you are in a weak state of mind or body, you may serve education best by just returning a set of papers unread the next day. This is better than coming to class all worn out from sitting up all night correcting papers and feeling like a martyr. As I said, it takes a saint to live with a martyr, and it's not realistic to expect our students to be saints. When I use this method with a set of papers, I always tell students what I did and why, and they understand.

A note on late papers and marks

Without doubt, handing in papers late is a bad habit. Some teachers "mark down" late papers. That to me has always seemed to be misleading, if we are really serious about our policy that marks are information. I suggest, instead, the following procedure for late papers.

• Tell the class in advance that handing in papers when they are due is important for three reasons: people should learn to be punctual; it's usually better for the class if all the papers are evaluated together; and it's more convenient for you, the teacher. When papers come in late, you will mark them "late" and make a note of the fact in your gradebook.

• Tell students that even the best of us sometimes can't meet deadlines, and encourage them, if they are up against more than they can get done, to talk it over with you. Promise to be understanding as long as lateness doesn't get to be a habit. Point out, on the other hand, that planning one's time to get work done on schedule is important, and try to help students learn to do this.

• Mark all papers the same, whether handed in on time or not, since marks are information about qualities of the papers, not about when they were handed in. Never mark down for lateness.

• When writing a student's report, if several papers came in late during a marking period, note the fact as an important piece of information that may properly affect your evaluation of the student's overall performance.

24.
Keeping in Touch

> *Hint 91.* The amount of good accomplished by
> a thoughtful teacher in private conversations
> with his pupils is hard to estimate.
>
> *Abbie G. Hall*

One of my favorite stories about not being in touch with the feelings of other people is that of the eight-year-old girl and her small brother who were on the loose in the Neiman-Marcus department store in Dallas one hot afternoon. The children had bought ice cream cones and were amusing themselves by riding the escalators. They were jammed together with other passengers, and the boy, noticing that his cone was dripping, wiped it on the mink stole of the woman in front of him. His sister cried out, "Watch out, Johnny! You're getting fur all over your ice cream."

This epitomizes the human condition: we have great difficulty in seeing things from any point of view but our own. Teachers in any good school should, by example, precept, and planned experiences, train their students to put themselves in the situation of others, to see things from others' points of view, and, further, to explain to others their own point of view, situation, and feelings. We should constantly be teaching the art and science of keeping in touch with one another.

Teaching should not be just a one-way flow of information and directions from the full, dynamic teacher into the empty, docile student, but an exchange — sometimes quiet, sometimes lively — of ideas, questions, and points of view. A good school, or even a good classroom in a generally stiff and non-communicating school, offers lots of vital exchange and opportunities for the wearers of stoles and the eaters of ice cream cones to know one another.

Keeping in touch with students

John Holt, in *How Children Fail* (New York: Pitman, 1964), writes, "A teacher in a class is like a man in the woods at night with a powerful flashlight in his hand. Wherever he turns his light, the creatures on whom it shines are aware of it, and do not behave as they do in the dark. Thus the mere fact of his watching their behavior changes it into something very different. Shine where he will, he can never know very much of the night life of the woods." If our "watching" is like an intimidating beam of light in an otherwise dark room filled with frightened creatures, we had better look for some more general sources of light for all.

One source can be our own willingness to let our students see us as human beings with problems, frailties, and feelings, just like other people, and not simply as The Teacher. Openness on our part may beget openness on the part of our students. This doesn't mean "inflicting personal opinions on the class," or "crying in class," to mention two traits that students say they object to, but it means not being "an old square goat" who "just wants the money."

What it means is admitting it when we're wrong, showing that we're feeling great or terrible on this day or that, revealing that we can be hurt or made to feel good by what our students say and do, and that we, too, miss deadlines, can't get to work, lose things, and often would rather play than work. We can exemplify — or at least not try too hard to hide — our humanity without becoming unprofessional. At the same time, we should take care not to indulge in excessive self-revelation or make our personal lives a preoccupation of the class. Simply saying, on occasion, "Let me tell you how that makes me feel," helps keep them in touch with us and opens them to putting us in touch with them.

The other side of it, of course, is for us to keep ourselves as informed and aware as we can be of the state of mind and emotions of our students, as well as of their academic progress or lack of it. Here are some suggestions, to add to those made in earlier chapters, for helping us to keep in touch.

• Some of us grind on through our lesson plans, our schemes, and our subjects, intent on *our* purposes and goals, until we have allowed ourselves to get out of touch with the lives and learning of our students. It is therefore a good idea, from time to time, to stop and ask, "How are things going?" or "Is anything bothering anybody?" — and then listen.

• Sometimes it is better to hand out a sheet for students to fill out anonymously, reporting on their concerns and reactions. It can be as simple as this:

How Are Things Going?
1. With you and this class?
2. With my teaching?
3. Any suggestions for me?
4. Anything I should know about you? About others?

• Dealing with group problems in class meetings and with individual problems by talking with students can result in useful communication. At times, though, it is good simply to help students get their feelings out into the open. Child psychologist Dorothy Walter Baruch, in her book *New Ways in Discipline* (New York: McGraw-Hill, 1949), says that parents and teachers unconsciously tend to belittle the feelings of their children and students, starting at a very early age: "It doesn't hurt very much" (when it hurts a lot), "You don't really mind missing the party; you'll have lots of other chances" (when you really feel terrible about missing it), "Why, we all *love* the baby and are *glad* we have him!" Dr. Baruch says you should not tell people they don't feel what they know they feel, and you rarely should censor the expression of feelings, because that doesn't change them or eliminate them; it just drives them underground, where they can do a lot of harm. Rather, she says, feelings should be accepted, never condemned. Accepting and understanding a person's feelings is one way of keeping communications open. When anyone is being difficult and unpleasant, it usually doesn't help to cheer them, forbid them, condemn them, or reason with them, because such actions ignore the feelings. Help get the feelings out; then try the reasoning. Teachers should accept their students' feelings, but they don't have to accept all their actions. You can try to make it clear that people are not responsible for their feelings, but they are responsible — or should be — for their actions. They cannot control their feelings; they can learn to control their actions.

• Try to make yourself available for students to talk to, even though in most schools there simply isn't time, unless you open your class periods sometimes to allow it. But it's not only a question of being available; it's also a question of being talk-to-able. When I asked 400 students in grades 5-9, "Is it difficult for you to talk satisfactorily with your teachers about questions important to you?" 22 per cent said "Yes," 44 per cent said "At times," and 34 percent said "No." Then I asked, "If it is difficult, why?" Some of their answers are instructive. Fifth and sixth graders said, "She doesn't have time, the room's not very private, and she often doesn't understand a word I say," "They're too busy," "I'm shy," "I'm afraid," "They're not my father or mother." Students in grades 7-9 said, "They don't care," "They'd get mad and yell," "They don't really listen," "They're always right," "I've never considered talking to a teacher about anything," "I wouldn't want them to know about me."

• Before and after classes, during recess, in the morning and afternoon, as you work at your desk, listen to the student chitchat — not eavesdropping, just taking in the scene.

• A good way to learn indirectly how students are feeling and what they are thinking is to use the technique of role playing. It not only helps you to keep in touch with them but helps them to communicate with one another and with others outside. For example, after a fight over a serious difference of opinion, or self-interest, has cooled down, ask the antagonists to try to take each other's point of view and defend it in an argument. If it's too heated for them to do so, ask two other students to play the roles of the antagonists and then let the class discuss the actions and words. Occasionally, you can take part in role playing, too: you can be one of the student antagonists, or ask a student to play you and you play a type of student who annoys you, and then discuss the role play. Role playing is usually a fairly painless, often very funny, way of bringing out truths and forces that would be too painful to talk about directly.

• If you can get a visiting day, spend it in your own school following the program — *all day* — of students in a class you teach. It is amazing what a variety of circumstances, personalities, standards of discipline, and expectations that students adjust to with seeming success. In a way, they are like water poured into vessels of different shapes; they take on the shape of each vessel and adjust; not often do they spill or boil over.

• Keep in touch with your students by maintaining good records in your own record book so that you can remind yourself at a glance where each student is, at least in some important respects. How much and what kinds of information you keep are pretty much up to you.

Keeping in touch with colleagues

In some schools, some teachers pour all their being into their own classroom-castles, to which they repair at start of day and from which they flee at the end, meeting colleagues only at faculty meetings, in the hall, and, if necessary, at lunch.

In other schools, the teachers are the center of one another's social lives, and they meet, eat, gossip, picnic, drink, study, and party together, sometimes joyfully, sometimes with the grim purpose of knowing one another in every dimension and thus of improving. It's fine for teachers to be friends and socialize if they enjoy it and it happens easily, but most of us will be better teachers if we reserve a good hunk of our lives for the normal world outside of school and if we try to keep in touch with the main currents of life.

Even so, within the school day and on the school premises, there are many ways by which we can and should keep in touch with one another for our own sakes and for the sakes of our students.

• Do talk shop. What could be more interesting, if you like your work, than talking about it? I've never understood why people feel they have to say, "Excuse me for talking shop, but . . ."

• Use the lunch table as a ready-made, effortless occasion for sharing ideas and working out the hundreds of little coordinations and passings of information that make schools work well. It's even all right to compare notes on individual students, provided they are not nearby and provided you aren't just gossiping. Gossip is illegitimate communication in schools.

• The faculty room is an even better place than lunch to let your hair down and express your pleasures, worries, and frustrations. Where else could a teacher say about reincarnation, at the end of a long, hard day, "Well, if there's anything to it, I want to come back as a childhood disease"?

• Visit your colleagues' classes and invite them to visit yours. It is good if a school's staff members can be open enough with one another to be able to enter and leave classrooms without its being an event. A few five-minutes glimpses can often provide more healthy material for communication than an entire 45-minute period sat dutifully all the way through. After the visits, you can compare notes. Through visits, you can give and receive ideas, approaches, and methods for working with students and subjects that weeks of faculty meetings do not provide.

• Use free periods you may have in common with other teachers to plan and talk. Never assume, though, that just because a teacher is sitting alone in an empty room he or she is available. Ask first, before plunging in.

• Try to schedule an occasional meeting of all the teachers of a given grade to compare notes and to discuss especially difficult students or students who need more challenge — and don't forget all the great undiscussed.

• Never encourage, even with the best of motives, a whole class to talk with you or in your presence about their objections to and difficulties with another teacher. You may want to listen just long enough to get the gist of the problem, in case you can think of a way to help the teacher, but almost always the best policy is to tell your students, "Talk it over with Mr. X. After all, it's you and he who have to work it out." If you know Mr. X well enough, you can, with due caution and hesitation, tell him what seems to be coming up and what you said to the class.

• And a word about faculty meetings — among the best places to communicate and among the worst. They are best when faculty and administration plan the agenda together; when substantive issues come first and little announcements last, when people are too weary to quibble over them; when everybody feels free to say what is on his or her mind; and when the goal is not to win points or to prevail but to reach a consensus by which all can work constructively. Faculty meetings are at their worst when they turn into gripe sessions; when they are devoted to scolding or to pep talks; and when most people can't wait to get out of the meeting to say what they really think. Make it a rule to say it in the meeting, if it's important, or not to say it at all — at least for 48 hours, and then to say it to someone who can help solve rather than aggravate the problem.

Keeping in touch with "the administration"

John Coleman, former president of Haverford College, said, "In actuality, a president is at the center of a web of conflicting interest groups, none of which can ever be fully satisfied. He is, by definition, almost always wrong. . . . It's all very interesting, and not hard to take once he gets over wanting to be right and settles instead for doing the best he can." Coleman could just as well have been talking about school principals, most of whom find it a mighty challenge to reach the state of maturity that he describes.

I spent four years as a school principal, but after about two I knew I wanted to get out of the job and back to the real rewards of teaching. Hardly anyone told me that I was doing a good job — and I tried very hard — until I announced my intention to resign.

The best way to keep in touch with "the administration" is to try to understand what their lives are like. It seems to me that school heads and principals often are perceived by teachers and students as being relatively rich; protected from the daily grind and pressures by a competent secretary; inhabiting a spacious, well-furnished office on the quiet side of the school; consorting with the movers and shakers, usually at lunch off the premises; keeping for themselves those things they like to do and delegating everything else; enjoying the exercise of power; and not having any papers to mark in the evenings.

Consider the following facts about the lives of principals.

They don't have the luxury of shooting off their mouths because what they say is heard as The Institution Speaking. They aren't allowed to complain; it's too catching.

They get to know hundreds of people slightly and few people intimately. Everybody knows them, but they can't know everybody, even though they are expected to.

They rarely get easy problems to solve. Only the toughest ones reach their desks. They have to make hundreds of small decisions quickly, and with inadequate evidence, for often making no decision is worse than making an imperfect one, or is, in itself, a decision.

They have to hear all sides and suspend judgment while advocates, complainers, and demands for action (or for stopping action) press upon them. Their brains and desks are a tangle (or an ordered web) of suspended judgments. They have to conduct an orchestra of cacophonous interests and concerns and often compose the score while conducting. They must hear cacophony but broadcast only harmony.

Most of their problems never go away; they just have to be dealt with in new forms. Thus heads risk feeling like the frustrated Australian who got a new boomerang and spent the rest of his life trying to throw the old one away.

They have to give credit to others for all the good things that happen and take or expect no credit for themselves. Conversely, if something goes wrong, from furnace to advanced calculus, it's their fault — or someone thinks it is.

They have to be ready to say something on all public occasions, thus running the deadly professional hazard of not recognizing that they don't have anything to say.

Since no one can imagine they need it, they receive very little praise and encouragement. They can never say their work is done.

For a really good school head or principal, I'm sure the main reward is the inner satisfaction that comes from giving one's all and feeling that, on the whole, the job is well done. But heads are human, and occasionally they need praise and encouragement.

They need to be told they've done a good job when they have — "That was a good, witty speech and right to the point," "The new science teacher told me what a great help your visit was and how many good ideas she got from it."

They need to be shown that their colleagues recognize that their life is tough — "I don't see how you manage to keep so much in mind the way you do," "I know you had a meeting

this morning and have a meeting tonight, so I'll be brief,"
"Johnny X complained about the messy classrooms, and I
thought you ought to know, since Mrs. X talks all over."

They need to hear someone in a faculty or parents' meeting
speaking the truth about a problem and suggesting a solution
based on the needs of the entire school, now and future, with
good humor and caring, without any ego involved.

And they need to have someone available, either in school or
outside, with whom they can be utterly honest, unpremedi-
tated, tentative, troubled, distressed, or exultant, knowing that
what is said will be passed on to no one — but no one.

I have two other suggestions for keeping in touch with the
administration.

Do not assume that, just because their doors are closed, administrators are not willing to see you. If you have a concern
you wish to share, make an appointment, preferably for a day
or two hence so that you can be sure it's worth talking about.
Don't storm the door in anger and go away feeling rejected.
When making your appointment, write a short note explaining
what you want to talk about so that the administrator can
prepare for your conference.

Invite administrators to visit your classes.

A word about trustees and school boards

Mark Twain defined school boards as "what God made, after
he practiced by making idiots." (Twain also said that "truth is
a rare commodity, and therefore should be used sparingly.")

Too many of us cut ourselves off psychologically from the
boards that govern our schools by assuming that they could
somehow, if they really wanted to, establish the policies and
especially provide the money to solve the problems of the
school we are in. It's a careless sort of luxury to blame board
members for school problems and inadequacies, which they are
probably very much aware of and are trying to grapple with.

One of the most unwise actions a teacher can take, unless
members of the faculty are expressly invited to do so, is to get
into private conversation with a trustee about a specific opera-
tional matter. If you feel that there is something that the
school board or the trustees really need to know and do not

know, speak about it first with the head of your school or someone else on the staff who meets with the board. After that, if you still feel that the board needs to hear from you, ask the head how best to go about being heard.

The other side of the coin is that board members should never get involved in the daily operations of the school (beyond making a suggestion on a take-it-or-leave-it basis). The line between determination of policy and daily operation of the school should be clearly drawn.

Board members should be encouraged to visit the school, to observe classes, and to talk with students and teachers about what is going on in the school so that they will gain the background they need when called upon to develop and determine policy. You as a teacher can help in this by encouraging those you know to come and see.

25.
Ignorance in Stilts?

The eighteenth-century poet William Cowper, who was bullied in early life at a private school, published in 1785 a six-book poem called *The Task*. Of the many things that Cowper was against, one was the wrong sort of schools, about which, in *The Task*, he wrote:

> The schools become a scene
> Of solemn farce, where Ignorance in stilts,
> His cap well lin'd with logic not his own,
> With parrot tongue perform'd the scholar's part,
> Proceeding soon a graduated dunce.

In how many of our classrooms today is what goes on a solemn farce? In how many of them does the thinking — not the student's but the teacher's — get in only as far as the student's cap? How many recitations are parrot-tongued as if performing a part rather than participating in some sort of reality? And from how many of our schools do graduated dunces proceed, high IQ score or low?

What sorts of people would we like to send forth from our schools? A great and strong variety, of course; people who feel good about themselves; people who can consider others; and people who can read. Perhaps those are the minimum essentials. But I should like to go farther and suggest some other characteristics of people that I believe the world needs.

We need people who are critical thinkers, who won't accept anything unthinkingly. This is difficult to achieve because students tend to exercise their critical thinking on what is around them — school, classes, teachers, parents.

We need people who are honest and forthright, even uncomfortably so. Too many of us tend to be too tactful, too afraid to state our convictions. I don't mean we should encourage brutal forthrightness, for you can tell the truth unkindly, and there is even some truth that doesn't need to be spoken at all. But much more often it is better to speak the truth as we see it and to encourage students to do so. We need people who keep trying to communicate, to explain, to find out what others think, and to say what they think and feel.

We need people who will persist in the faith that good will and intelligence, applied by caring, informed people who are moved by their consciences, can improve any situation, whether in a person's life, in a community, or in the world. Schools work primarily on the brain, and we need people who show, in the words of landscape architect Ian McHarg, that the human brain is the apex of evolution on spaceship Earth and not a recently blossomed spinal tumor. And, as anthropologist and poet Loren Eiseley said, in *Not Man Apart* (San Francisco: California-Based Friends of the Earth, 1977), "The need is not really for more brains, the need is now for a gentler, a more tolerant people than those who won for us against the ice, the tiger, and the bear. The hand that hefted the axe, out of the same old blind allegiance to the past, fondles the machine gun as lovingly. It is a habit man will have to break to survive, but the roots go very deep." We need people who can use their brains — with gentleness and tolerance.

We need people who take evil, wrongdoing, and injustice personally when these are done to others and who react also when these are done to them. We should train our students to get involved in trying to right injustice, not to pass it by on the other side. We want people who have a chronic social conscience.

We need people who are willing to be unpopular or in the minority, not just for the fun of it, but because what the majority of people are doing usually needs criticism and improvement. But such an attitude should be held without self-righteousness. We need people who will admit that they are wrong.

We need people who, if they have privileges — material, social, mental, physical — feel uncomfortable unless these privileges and powers are harnessed to use for others. Someone said that our duty should be to comfort the afflicted and to afflict the comfortable.

We need people who are not just tolerant of those who are different but who appreciate them, who go out of their way to cross barriers, whether economic, social, racial, or national.

We need people whose loyalty is primarily to the world, not to the nation, for we have reached a point where we must see the welfare of all human beings as inextricably mixed. Loyalty to the world is all very fine, but the place we need people to act and work for improvement is where they actually find themselves. It may be interesting to consider what the Chinese, the Russians, the Arabs, the Ugandans, or the Israelis should be doing, but we need people who act primarily as enlightened citizens of their own community, state, and nation. In that sense, we need patriots.

We need people who are religious, people concerned with the world of the spirit, the world of nonphysical things — love and humor, intellect, sweetness, friendship, loyalty, talk, ideals, and ideas — all things that you can't hold in your hand. *Religio* has to do with linking things together, finding out how they all bind together. To develop that sort of religion ought to be a concern of all schools.

We need people who have a sense of unfinishedness. Just as we teachers should know that in any class we do not finish what we begin (or if we do, it was probably not worth beginning), so our students should know that their education does not end with school, and we should try to communicate to them a continuing zest for learning and allow them to experience that zest with us. A third-grade girl once asked her teacher, "Do I now know half as much as I don't know?" What a wonderful question from the happy state of mind of a third grader, who thought that somehow, some day, she was really going to know everything.

But the truth is that knowledge — all kinds of knowledge, whether factual or spiritual — is like an island in an infinite sea of unknown. The larger the island becomes, the longer is its coastline bordering on the sea of the unknown. The more we know, the more we are in touch with what we don't know. And that is an important attitude for all of us to hold. Otherwise, we may be encouraging mere ignorance in stilts.

Appendix

Points Picked Up: One Hundred Hints
in How To Manage a School
by
Abbie G. Hall

This little book is made up of gleanings from many school journals, educational books and talks with other teachers spreading over many years of teaching. It seems to me that if I, at the beginning of my work, had had a friend to instruct me, give me hints, or to tell me what in the educational books and school journals would be of practical use to me I'd have saved much time and some annoying experiences. I hope these "Points Picked Up" will be to you, young teachers, the words of a friend. — The Author

1. Begin school as if you had just heard good news and took pleasure in imparting, and keep this up all day.
2. If you would keep a bright pupil out of mischief give him enough to do.
3. To teach is not to simplify every step until there is no real work for the child to do.
4. Many children, if they learn good breeding at all, must learn it at school, so endeavor to make school the district center of good manners and politeness.
5. Get the parents to visit school even if you have to resort to giving exhibitions in which their children "show off."
6. In an ungraded school have the smallest possible number of classes and in classification consider both age and capacity.
7. Train your older pupils to correct and credit the papers of younger ones.
8. If your school is large, alternate the recitations of the more advanced. Do not attempt to hear all the classes every day.

Points Picked Up was No. 2 in the Ways and Means Series, published in Chicago in 1891 by A. Flanagan, Publisher.

9. Teach the book. Many teachers express dissatisfaction with the book. If you can find a better one, use that. If you cannot find a better one and think you can write a better one — write it. But if you can do neither, teach the one you have so that the pupil may have something to rely upon when he cannot have you. Do not depend upon blackboard or oral teaching entirely.

10. The "thank you's" and "if you please's" are important items in school discipline.

11. Every thing that is explained to a pupil which he can find out for himself robs him of so much education.

12. To aid in discipline — Mark each section daily, giving the sections perfect in deportment a yellow mark (call it a gold mark). The imperfect sections receiving white marks. At the end of the week the section having the most "good marks" is entitled to certain privileges for a week — such as being dismissed first, etc.

13. Another — Elect captains of sections and let them choose pupils to sit in their sections. If a section is perfect in deportment all day, place 100 merits to its credit on the board. At the end of the week or fortnight elect new captains and choose over. The pupils who have lowered the grade of their sections will find themselves very unpopular.

14. Another — Establish a system of bookkeeping. Each pupil keeping his own account of Dr. and Cr. A failure or misdemeanor being entered on the Dr. side and each perfect day in deportment on the Cr. side. At the end of the week they must balance their books and report.

15. This is an old device, but a useful one for saving noise and confusion: Establish a system of signs by means of which the pupil may ask the teacher from his place in his seat and without speaking. For example: — Raising one finger may mean "May I come to you?" Two fingers "May I speak?" Three fingers — "May I pass to some other part of the room?" etc.

16. To do away with noise when passing out — Appoint monitors to bring wraps, etc., to their owners and let them be put on a few moments before dismissal. While this is being done a song may be sung or you or a pupil be reading some entertaining story aloud. Your noisiest pupil will forget to be noisy.

17. A teacher who has to resort to repeated calling his school to order by tinkling the bell or by speaking, lacks the art of good management.

18. Whispering — Have a talk with the pupil about the trouble it makes — 1. Robbing another of his time. 2. How speaking of important things soon runs into the habit of talking of unimportant. 3. That even a little whispering disturbs those in his neighborhood. 4. How it

calls the teacher's attention from the classes. 5. Finally — how it interferes with the working order of the entire school. Such a talk is often effective. Try to make it *unpopular* to whisper.

19. To keep desks neat — Near the beginning of the term take time to have books placed in order, one by one, according to the teacher's directions. This establishes an order to be followed throughout the year.

20. It is a temptation when a pupil is in trouble with his lesson to help him out with it, but it certainly is a mistake on the teacher's part to give any help until his pupil has first made an earnest attempt to help himself.

21. Some teachers actually discourage their pupils by expecting too much of them.

22. No teacher should be continually saying to his pupils, "You will surely fail on examination with such lessons as these," "You are doing poorly," etc. It irritates both pupil and teacher.

23. The cases are rare indeed when ridicule has good results and the teacher who desires good work should avoid it under all circumstances.

24. Nothing is surer than that pupils grow and develop by what they do themselves, not by what their teacher does for them, therefore; he is the most successful teacher who gets the most work out of his pupils, not he who works the most himself.

25. Often the reason a pupil has difficulty in learning a lesson from a book is that he is not able to read it. See that each child *reads* his grammar, geography and arithmetic understandingly.

26. When something funny occurs in school don't be afraid to laugh. It is frequently better to laugh than to scold.

27. Choose certain places on your blackboard for certain lessons, and, by habitually following this rule, the children will come to know where to look for instructions as to each lesson.

28. Blackboard, crayon, books, pointers, pencils, maps, etc., are the teacher's tools. The convenient and orderly arrangement of these tools will save time and, also, every day teach an object lesson in orderly habits.

29. Write every morning, in a conspicuous place on the blackboard, a new motto.

30. Never at any time give a pupil information without expecting him, at some future time, to give it back.

31. Be in the district, if possible, a few days before school opens.

32. Organize the older pupils of your school into a reading club, meeting weekly or monthly.

33. A query box, into which questions on morals and manners are

placed by pupils, for the teacher to answer, often brings a needed reform in that line. The reading and answering the questions may be part of the opening exercises.

34. Don't waste time in the class having things explained that are well understood.

35. Don't wander too much from the lesson.

36. Don't waste time by attempting to explain to the children what is entirely beyond their comprehension.

37. Don't have children fold their arms. It is uncomfortable and makes them crooked.

38. See to the orderly arrangement of everything. Have a place for each pupil to hang up his hat, keep his books and sit in the class.

39. Have as few classes as consistent with the wants of the school.

40. Begin promptly and close promptly.

41. Use suggestions instead of commands.

42. Make few rules.

43. See that the room is properly ventilated.

44. Try to govern by the eye rather than by the voice.

45. Keep the dull and idle pupils in front.

46. Don't neglect the quiet, dull children. Often a child is neglected simply because he is good, that is, he makes no disturbance and the teacher does not find out how little he is learning until examination comes.

47. Don't neglect the bashful child. Often he does not comprehend and his timidity prevents his asking for explanation.

48. Four essential qualifications of a good teacher: 1. Pure and upright moral character. 2. Scholarship. 3. Ability to impart instruction. 4. Good governing powers.

49. Never deprive a child of anything of value without returning it to him at the proper time.

50. Do not encourage pupils to report each other's misdemeanors.

51. Never find fault without showing why and indicating a better way.

52. Be slow to promise but quick to perform.

53. Ask yourself "Would I like to go to school to such a teacher as I am?"

54. Discipline should aim at improving the character.

55. The teacher should be an example in person and character of what he requires of his pupils.

56. Studies should be adapted to the capacity of the pupils.

57. Scholars should not be kept in at recess. It is not play alone that those so detained are deprived of, but of that necessary physical exercise and relaxation from mental application which the young so require.

58. Scholars should not be detained after school hours as punishment or to make up deficient lessons. They belong to you only during school hours, after that your authority ceases. It is doing yourself a wrong as well as the children. You are both tired, mentally and physically, and it is your *duty* to go home and let the child go too.

59. Write the following on the blackboard and see what the children say about it:

My Duty as a Pupil

1. Attention to my teacher's instruction.
2. Good behavior at all times.
3. Not to communicate during school hours.
4. Not to present as my own any work that is done by others.
5. Not to laugh at trifles and create disturbance.
6. Not to ridicule new methods introduced into the school room.
7. To be prompt in obeying signals.
8. To remember that if I act in an unbecoming manner it reflects upon my bringing up at home.
9. To use my best endeavors to influence the younger pupils for good.
10. To do all of to-day's work to-day.
11. To study politeness and keep in mind that it pays to exercise it.

60. *Think* about your work; *talk* about it only when necessary.

61. Attend all the teacher's meetings you possibly can.

62. There are two ways in which teachers injure and ill-use memory. They give it no variety of work or they refuse all exercise whatever.

63. Don't have too much blackboard work. It ruins many children's eyes.

64. The teacher's success depends in a great measure upon pleasing the people. This does not depend altogether upon methods of teaching. First please the pupils.

65. A teacher's social qualities often have more to do with his success than the excellence of his methods.

66. "John" or "Mary" can spoil any teacher's popularity in the district, therefore, in as far as you conscientiously can, keep "John" and "Mary's" good will.

67. Greet pupils pleasantly when they arrive in the morning. Help the little ones to get off their wraps and to the fire.

68. Accept invitations to the homes of the pupils or to parties in the neighborhood.

69. Talk with parents about their children and use as much praise as will not injure your conscience.

70. Try to send the children home with favorable reports of your work as a teacher. Don't despise these little advertisements if deserving.

71. Try to unite with the teachers of your neighborhood for the general good.

72. School directors will always help a teacher who helps herself.

73. Be reasonably polite to your pupils but do not be officious.

74. If there are any grumblers in your district do not turn a cold shoulder on them. Go to them and try to find the basis of their discontent — they frequently have one.

75. Among the minor ways of securing punctuality and regular attendance is to have a part of the blackboard reserved for absent and tardy pupils to write their names on when they return.

76. Another scheme for the tardy: — Have a board on which the pupils' names are written (opposite each name a hole being drilled), hung in a convenient position. Have a box at hand containing both black and white pegs. When a pupil arrives in time he sticks a white peg opposite his name. If tardy a black one. This also makes a convenient device for calling the roll.

77. Another — Have both red and blue ribbon badges. At the end of the week give the pupil who has been neither absent nor tardy a blue ribbon, those who have been tardy, only, a red one, those absent receive nothing.

78. Questions like the following put on the board occasionally for the older pupils to answer will set them to thinking and perhaps do more good than a course of lectures on morality.

1. What trait of character do you dislike most?
2. What one do you admire most?
3. What character in American history do you admire most?
4. What one do you dislike most?
5. Give reasons for these likes and dislikes.
6. What quality do you admire most in a man?
7. In a woman?
8. What do you regard as the greatest source of evil?
9. Who is your favorite novelist?
10. Who is your favorite poet?
11. What is your favorite novel?
12. What is your favorite poem?

79. Give as few orders as possible but be firm in having them promptly and thoroughly obeyed when given.

80. Try to impress children with due respect to law.

81. Good discipline is impossible with children unemployed. Allow no waste of time in beginning.

82. Avoid speaking in a loud, blustering tone.

83. Be ever on the alert and warn when necessary.

84. Do not scold and never threaten.

85. Give careful attention to details.

86. Know your boys.

87. Never sneer at children. Be cautious not to dampen their natural ardor and gaiety.

88. Authority should be felt not seen.

89. The need for much punishment means, in nearly all cases, weak handling. If children are troublesome look to yourself first.

90. In teaching, distinguish carefully between the means and the end.

91. The amount of good accomplished by a thoughtful teacher in private conversations with his pupils is hard to estimate.

92. What constitutes good order depends upon circumstances. What would be good order in a high school might be very poor in a primary just because it would be too good and obtained by too much constraint and repression.

93. In the lower grades never tell pupils to study until you have told them what to do and how to do it.

94. Give short lessons to young pupils but give them a good deal to do about each.

95. Have the school room well ventilated (by opening windows at top and bottom, if necessary). Impure air enervates both leader and children and sows the seeds of disease.

96. Sweeping should be done after school, never in the morning.

97. A teacher's success is often measured by his ability to advance small pupils.

98. Keep pupils busy and you will easily control them. When you assign them work see that they do it.

99. Show an interest in your pupils; fix up a neat school room for them and you will not be under the necessity of searching for a new school each year.

100. Passing to class or from the room: — Ask the members of the class to rise at a given signal; if any one hesitates or gets up slowly, have all sit, give signal, and rise again. Repeat this in a pleasant way until all rise at the same time. When this is accomplished, agree upon a signal for passing. If pupils pass abruptly, or out of order, try to show them how to pass quietly, then require this, in a pleasant manner, until the object is attained.

101. When pupils persist in crowding and pushing when passing from the room, notice carefully those who do not crowd; mention their names, and say that they may rise and pass out together at the

first signal and say that the others need more time because they get so confused and disorderly; for the present they may go last; but as fast as they learn to be orderly and soldier-like they may join the ranks.

102. If you notice your pupils unusually restless and inattentive, allow them to spend a moment in some simple physical exercise.

103. Have occasionally pronunciation lists. Select and put on the board about ten words commonly mispronounced. Do this in time to enable earnest pupils to consult the dictionary.

104. Do not distract attention. It is wrong to stop the work of a class because one pupil is a little disorderly at his seat.

105. A teacher is responsible for the proper care of the school property in his charge.

106. The teacher should especially guard against having such a rush of work come to a focus at the hour of closing that the school shall be dismissed in confusion. Better call all work to a close a few minutes before the time for dismissal, and have all pass out quietly and in order.

107. Whispering: — Ask the pupils to go without whispering for half an hour or an hour and at the end of the time ascertain who have succeeded, letting them raise their hands. Commend their success, give them a little rest, and then let them try for another period.

108. Whispering: — Have a time set apart for speaking, by having a large card marked "Study Hour" on one side and "Needful Speech" on the other. At the end of each hour turn the card with the "Needful Speech" out for a minute.

109. Whispering: — Keep an eye on the noisy ones and give them a separate place to sit, not so much as a punishment as to prevent them from disturbing others.

110. Whispering: — Give extra employment to those who seem to have time for whispering.

111. Whispering: — Dismiss in order or orderly conduct as you have noted it.

113 [sic]. Do not punish when angry.

112. Do not let a known fault go unpunished but do not magnify small offences.

113. If about to enter a strange school room do not imagine strange things. Your ideal *concept* of a school room and the room you enter will not tally.

114. If a record has been kept by your predecessor, study it carefully.

115. Set down as one of your first day's tasks to get acquainted with the *names* of your pupils. It gives you a hold upon them.

116. Honor your School Board that your days may be long in the land in which you are teaching.

Index